HEROES OF HISTORY

BILLY GRAHAM

America's Pastor

HEROES OF HISTORY

BILLY GRAHAM

America's Pastor

JANET & GEOFF BENGE

Emerald Books

P.O. BOX 635, LYNNWOOD, WA 98046

Emerald Books are distributed through YWAM Publishing. For a full list of titles, including other great biographies, visit our website at www.emeraldbooks.com.

Billy Graham: America's Pastor
Copyright © 2014 by Janet and Geoff Benge

Published by Emerald Books
P.O. Box 635
Lynnwood, Washington 98046

Second printing 2018

Library of Congress Cataloging-in-Publication Data is available from the publisher and the Library of Congress.

ISBN 978-1-62486-024-9 (paperback)
ISBN 978-1-62486-026-3 (e-book)

Printed in the United States of America

HEROES OF HISTORY
Biographies

Available in paperback, e-book, and audiobook formats.
Unit Study Curriculum Guides are available for each biography.
www.emeraldbooks.com

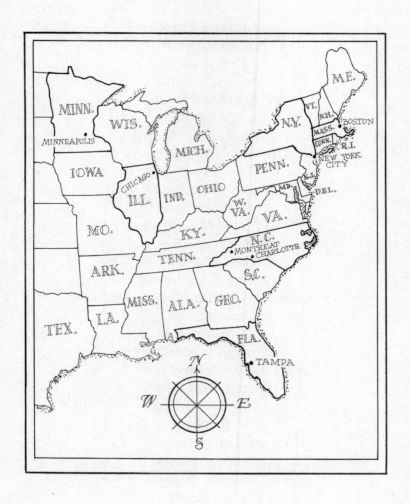

Contents

Chapter 1

On the Farm

B illy Frank, someone's here to take you and your sister home. You're dismissed."

Billy Frank looked at his teacher. Could this be true? Class had just returned from morning recess, and now he and his sister Catherine were being picked up to go home. Billy Frank frowned. Nothing like this had happened before in his twelve years of life. Had something gone wrong at the farm? Were his parents all right?

The eyes of the other students in the class were fixed on Billy Frank as he picked up his lunch pail and walked out of the classroom. Catherine, who was two years younger, looked concerned as she joined her brother at the Woodlawn School gate.

"Look, Reese is here to get us," Catherine said, referring to their father's right-hand man on the farm. "What do you think has happened?"

Billy Frank shrugged his shoulders. "I hope it's nothing bad."

When the Model A Ford came to a halt in front of them, the two Graham children climbed in. Billy Frank took the front seat beside Reese Brown.

"What's happened, Reese?" Billy Frank asked as they pulled away from the school.

Reese reached out his large black hand and tousled Billy Frank's sandy blond hair. "I reckon it's all right to tell you," he said. "You'll find out soon enough. The doc just visited and says your grandmother has only a few hours to live."

Billy Frank watched the rolling hills of Mecklenburg County, North Carolina, go by as he took in the news. His mother's mother, Grandma Coffey, was the only grandparent he'd known. The others had died before he was born. He liked his grandmother. She was old and often talked about the war—the American Civil War, not the Great War in Europe that had ended the same week Billy Frank was born.

"Don't worry. She's on her way to heaven," Catherine said with the matter-of-factness of a ten-year-old girl.

Billy Frank nodded. He knew quite a bit about heaven. His older sister Margaret had died as a baby, and his mother often talked about how they would all be reunited one day. For a boy his age, Billy Frank had certainly heard enough sermons on the subject. Each Sunday morning his family attended the Associated Reformed Presbyterian Church five miles away in Charlotte. There the Reverend Lindsay preached sermon after sermon without ever smiling.

Sometimes Billy Frank wondered why Mr. Lindsay hadn't decided to become an undertaker instead of a minister. He certainly had the temperament for it.

Billy Frank had been thinking a lot lately about how things at church were so dreary. The only songs they sang were psalms set to music. Even though he was leader of the youth group, Billy Frank hadn't been able to find a way to make that interesting either. He also realized that his mother was more interested in Christianity than his father was. His mother, Morrow Graham, was the one who made the children get ready for church and sit still during the service. And if the family could not attend church on Sunday night because the cows had to be milked, she would gather Billy Frank, Catherine, and their younger brother, Melvin, together around the kitchen table and read them a Bible story.

As the Model A turned the corner onto Park Road, Billy Frank craned his neck to see whose car was parked outside their two-story brick house. He could see his uncle Tom's Buick and another car that he did not recognize. Although Billy Frank knew he should be feeling sad, he was also secretly happy when he thought about all the cousins who would gather for the funeral. The Graham family lived on three hundred acres of gently rolling farmland, which his father and uncle had inherited from their father. Billy Frank hoped he would have time to take his cousins into the woods to show them his Tarzan hideout. Catherine laughed at his attempts to swing from vines, but Billy Frank felt he was getting closer to perfecting his technique.

When the car pulled to a stop in front of the house, Billy Jr., Billy Frank's big red goat came running out to meet them, followed by a gaggle of curious geese herded by six-year-old Melvin.

"Grandma's very sick. They think she's going to die," Melvin said as Billy Frank unwound his tall, thin body from the front seat.

"We know," Billy Frank said. "Reese told us."

The three Graham children climbed the front steps of the brick farmhouse, where their mother waited by the front door. She gave Billy Frank and Catherine each a hug. "Grandma's near the end of her earthly journey. It's time to say good-bye," their mother said, guiding the children toward the back bedroom.

In the bedroom lay Billy Frank's grandmother. She was breathing lightly, and her mouth gaped open. Billy Frank reached out and held her bony hand.

"It won't be long," his mother said.

In fact, Lucinda Coffey continued to breathe lightly, stopping every now and then, until late into the night. Billy Frank and his parents were in the room when the end came. All at once the calm mood was broken when Billy Frank's grandmother sat bolt upright as if she'd been struck by lightning. She declared, "I see Jesus. He has His arms outstretched toward me. And there's Ben! He has both of his eyes and both of his legs. They're coming for me!" She smiled and reached out her arms, then lay back on the pillow—dead.

Billy Frank sat in silence. He felt as if he had been struck by lightning himself. It seemed incredible that his grandmother had seen Jesus, along with his dead grandfather. Billy Frank would have liked to have seen him too. Granddaddy Benjamin Coffey was a legend in the area. With the rank of sergeant, he fought against the Yankees with Pettigrew's Brigade, part of the Eleventh North Carolina Regiment. The regiment had led the advance on Gettysburg from the west. In the ensuing fighting, Billy Frank's grandfather had been struck in the left leg with shrapnel. As he lay bleeding on the battlefield, a bullet grazed his right eye. He was taken to a field hospital and covered with a quilt that his aunt Hattie now proudly displayed in her living room. Benjamin Coffey had survived the ordeal, but his left leg was amputated, and he went blind in his right eye.

Billy Frank wished he'd known Granddaddy Coffey, who had died two years before Billy was born. But now, apparently, Grandma Coffey had seen him again, all fixed up with his leg regrown and his right eye working, coming with Jesus to get her. His grandmother seeing his grandfather just as she died was a lot to take in, but Billy Frank did not doubt it was true. Lucinda Coffey had been a staunch Presbyterian who never lied, even about the smallest of things. If she saw Billy Frank doing anything wrong, she always reminded him that God was watching. And now she was in heaven.

As Billy Frank lay in bed that night, he couldn't shake the image of his grandmother seeing both Jesus and her husband. Everything he'd been taught from the Bible was really true. He felt relieved, as he'd always been a little afraid of death. His mother had taught him the prayer, "Now I lay me down to sleep, I pray the Lord my soul to keep, and if I die before I wake, bless me, Lord, my soul to take." And every time he recited the prayer, Billy Frank felt nervous. He knew the words were intended to comfort a child, but they always made him wonder whether he would awake the next morning and where he might end up if he did not.

Following the funeral service on a cool morning in March 1931, the body of Grandma Lucinda Coffey was laid to rest beside her husband's in the church-yard of Steele Creek Presbyterian Church. Knowing that his grandmother was in heaven now made it easier for Billy Frank as he watched her coffin low-ered into the red dirt.

After the funeral Billy Frank and his cousins had plenty of time to practice their Tarzan stunts before Billy Frank had to milk the cows. This was a chore Billy Frank did every morning and afternoon, seven days a week. He didn't mind the afternoon milk-ing so much. He did that when he got home from school and needed some exercise after sitting at a desk all day. It was the morning milking that proved the most difficult, mainly because it involved waking up at two thirty a.m. Billy Frank was never ready to get up at that time. But his father was always up by then and expected his son to get straight up and do his chores.

After dressing, Billy Frank would head out of the house to wake Pedro, one of the farmhands, before going to the milking shed, where another farmhand already had the cows lined up in the stalls. Billy

Frank would take his three-legged stool and metal pail and begin his task of milking twenty of the cows. Two hours later he would be finished milking, and then it was time to shovel away the manure and feed the cows fresh hay. This was followed by the only part of this morning routine that Billy Frank really enjoyed—breakfast.

While the men were milking the cows, Morrow Graham and the maid chopped firewood, heated the stove, and cooked a hearty breakfast for them all. By the time Billy Frank made it to breakfast, he was always ready for a big helping of the grits and gravy, eggs, bacon, and rolls his mother had cooked. He washed it all down with a glass of fresh milk.

Having arisen so early, Billy Frank often had trouble concentrating on his schoolwork by the time morning recess rolled around. All he wanted to do was to sleep. Luckily, a good game of baseball at lunchtime would revive him for his afternoon classes.

Soon after Grandma Coffey's death, Billy Frank learned that there would be an addition to the Graham clan. At forty years of age, his mother was going to have another baby. Jean was born in the spring of 1932. At first Billy Frank found it difficult to think of her as his sister. He was now thirteen, and he calculated that he would leave home before Jean even got to first grade.

Just weeks after Jean's birth, tragedy struck the Graham family. Billy Frank was at school when once again he was pulled out of class. This time it was not Reese Brown who came to collect him but Pedro.

"What's happened?" Billy Frank asked Pedro as he climbed into the car.

Pedro shook his head and lowered his eyes. "It's your father."

Billy Frank felt panic rise in his throat. "Daddy? Is he d . . . dead?"

"No," Pedro said, "but he is in very bad shape."

"What happened?" Catherine asked from the backseat.

"Your father went into the woodshop to talk with Reese. Reese was using the mechanical saw to cut wood and turned around to hear what your daddy was saying. Must have loosened his grip on the wood, because the saw kicked up the wood, and it hit your daddy square in the jaw."

"Is he at home?" Billy Frank asked.

Pedro shook his head. "Took him straight to the hospital."

The rest of the way home Billy Frank stared out the window at the rolling fields of alfalfa. Random thoughts rushed through his head. What if his father died? Who would help Uncle Clyde run the Graham dairy farm? Would he have to leave school as soon as he turned fourteen to milk the cows? How would his mother go on without his daddy? To calm his thoughts, Billy Frank began to recite the Westminster Catechism to himself. It was something his mother had required he learn before his tenth birthday—107 questions and answers.

By the time they reached home, Billy Frank was up to the thirty-eighth question: *What benefits do believers receive from Christ at the resurrection?*

Answer: At the resurrection, believers, being raised up in glory, shall be openly acknowledged and acquitted in the day of judgment, and made perfectly blessed in the full enjoying of God to all eternity. As the car pulled to a halt, Billy Frank felt a chill go down his spine. Was that God's way of telling him his father was about to die and go to heaven?

Inside the Graham farmhouse the news was grim. Billy Frank's father lay in a coma in the hospital. His jaw had been shattered into many pieces and his head was cut open nearly to his brain. He had lost so much blood that he'd almost bled to death on the way to the hospital in the back of the old GMC truck.

The next week was pure agony for Billy Frank, who paced around the barn, begging God to save his father. His mother summoned her friends, and all day long prayer meetings were held in the house for Frank Graham's recovery. Sometimes the doctors sounded hopeful. Other times they talked about death being a mercy, since Frank would surely suffer brain damage if he lived.

By the end of the second week, the tide turned, and Frank's condition began to improve. It was a long, slow recovery, but after some time Billy Frank's father came home from the hospital and was able to do light duties around the farm. In time he made a full recovery, though Billy Frank had to get used to his father's face looking different. Frank's jaw had been set a little crooked, and he had several deep scars on his face. But there was something else different about him—Frank Graham had become much more interested in spiritual things.

Although the Graham family always went to church together, Billy Frank got the impression that this was more his mother's doing than his father's. But now things had changed. Frank Graham invited a group of Christian businessmen to hold a prayer rally on the farm. When he invited Billy Frank to join him at the prayer meeting, Billy Frank made an excuse. The last thing a teenage boy needed was for people at school to learn that he was hanging out with "holy rollers"!

Later that night Billy Frank overheard his father telling his mother how a man named Vernon Patterson had prayed at the prayer rally and asked God to raise up out of the Charlotte area someone to preach the gospel to the ends of the earth. Billy Frank wasn't so sure there was such a person in all of North Carolina, let alone the Charlotte area.

When Billy Frank was fifteen, his parents urged him to go with them to hear a visiting preacher named Dr. Mordecai Ham. Catherine and Melvin dutifully agreed to go with their parents, but Billy Frank had no interest in getting caught up in religious things. That changed when a friend of Billy Frank's, Albert McMakin, informed him that some of the students from Central High School in Charlotte were going to picket Mordecai Ham's meeting. "They say the preacher has no business telling them how to live their lives in this day and age. Prohibition's been lifted, and it's time to let people enjoy themselves. Don't you want to come along and see what happens?" Albert asked.

Billy Frank thought for a moment. Maybe he had misjudged the situation. Perhaps there would be more action at the meeting than at home.

"Come on," Albert urged. "Dad's been letting me drive the old vegetable truck into town. If you come, I'll let you drive."

That was all the encouragement Billy Frank needed. He'd get to see the high school students and the preacher in a showdown, and he'd drive the farm truck there and back as well. How could he resist?

Chapter 2

In the Line of Fire

Billy Frank took a second look as he pulled Albert's vegetable truck into the parking lot. Albert was seated beside him. Billy Frank had heard that Mordecai Ham drew large crowds to his meetings, but he'd never imagined anything quite like this. Hundreds of cars and trucks were parked in long rows. Thousands of people streamed into the huge steel and wood tabernacle that had been erected especially for the twelve weeks of meetings. Many carried large Bibles, and some seemed to be praying quietly to themselves as they walked. It reminded Billy Frank of the time his father had taken him to a Billy Sunday meeting when he was five years old.

Billy Sunday had been a center fielder for the Chicago White Stockings baseball team. Billy Frank remembered how hot it had been at the meeting and

how long Billy Sunday had preached. He remembered getting restless and his father telling him that
if he didn't settle down, Billy Sunday would yell his
name from the pulpit and a policeman would come
and arrest him. The memory made Billy Frank smile.
He'd always been a "mover," as his mother liked to
call it. In fact, his mother had once taken him to
the doctor to see if there was anything that could
be done about Billy Frank's constant need to be in
motion. The doctor just shook his head and said,
"He's perfectly normal, Mrs. Graham. It's just the
way he's built."

After climbing out of the truck, Billy Frank
looked around. Where were the students from Central High School in Charlotte? They were supposed
to be picketing Mordecai Ham's meeting. Billy Frank
had come to witness the action, but there appeared
to be none. Since there were no picketing students
to watch, Billy Frank decided to go in and see for
himself what Mordecai Ham was all about.

Billy Frank found a seat at the back of the tabernacle, a long way from where the preacher could
single him out. The meeting began with hymns. A
man named Walter Ramsay led the singing, and he
joked that he and Mordecai Ham were known as
"God's Ham and Ram Team." Billy Frank laughed.
Even though he could not sing in tune, he enjoyed
singing with a large crowd. He could sing as loudly
and off-key as he liked and not feel embarrassed.

When the last bar of the final hymn faded away,
Mordecai Ham stepped up to the podium. He looked
like a little old grandpa, with wire-rimmed glasses

and tufts of white hair framing the large bald spot on his head. But when he opened his mouth and began to speak, he sounded nothing like a little old grandpa. His voice boomed across the crowd as he used his finger to point forcefully out into the audience.

As he listened, Billy Frank thought every word and action of Dr. Ham was directed right at him. Dr. Ham preached from the Bible about how much God loved everyone and about the gift of eternal life offered through the death of Jesus Christ on the cross. Of course, Billy Frank had heard all this before. How could he not have? He'd been going to church since he was a baby, his parents prayed before every meal, Bible reading was held in his home after dinner each night, and his mother assigned the Graham children a Bible verse to memorize each day on the way to and from school. But somehow Mordecai Ham made these things sound different, and Billy Frank listened intently. On the drive back to the farm Billy Frank couldn't think about anything else but what the preacher had said, and he knew he wanted to hear more.

The next night Billy Frank was again seated in the tabernacle, and the night after that. He felt drawn to attend the meetings, yet at the same time Dr. Ham's sermons made him uncomfortable. Dr. Ham always talked about sin and rebelling against God, and Billy Frank felt the preacher was looking straight at him.

To be less in the line of fire of Mordecai Ham's words, Billy Frank volunteered to join the revival choir. That way, he figured, he could hear the sermons from a more comfortable spot behind the preacher.

On his first night in the choir, another teenage boy named Grady Wilson stood beside Billy Frank. Grady whispered to him, "I don't know what I'm doing here. One minute I was standing outside, and the next minute some old man grabbed me by the arm and told me to stand here. I feel like a fish out of water. I've never been in a choir before!"

Billy Frank grinned. "I haven't either. I can't sing a note. I'm just going to mouth the words. Do the same. We'll be fine."

Night after night the size of the crowd coming to the makeshift tabernacle grew. In his preaching, Dr. Ham talked about various types of sins, most of which Billy Frank had no experience with. There were others, though, that Billy Frank thought long and hard about. Mordecai Ham often railed against the evils of drinking alcohol. The Prohibition Amendment that made it illegal to sell, produce, or transport alcohol in the United States from 1920 to the early 1930s had been repealed the year before. And now that it was legal again, Billy Frank had tasted alcohol once—and hated it. He wondered if this consumption of alcohol counted as sin, since his father had given it to him and his sister Catherine. Billy Frank's father didn't drink alcohol at all, but when Prohibition ended he called the two elder Graham children into the kitchen, gave them each a bottle of beer, and ordered them to drink it all. Billy Frank gagged at the strong taste, and Catherine didn't do much better. By the time the bottles were empty both Billy Frank and Catherine swore they would never drink alcohol again. "Good," their father said.

"And from now on, whenever any of your friends try to get you to drink it, you tell them you've already tasted it and you don't like it."

Still, as the night meetings went on, Billy Frank began to understand that Mordecai Ham was preaching about other types of sins as well—more subtle sins, like the sin of pride. Billy Frank knew how that felt. He never prayed to ask God whether something was a good idea. He just went ahead and did what he thought seemed like the best thing to do.

And there was the sin of idolatry, which Dr. Ham said was allowing anything other than God to be the most important thing in your life. Immediately Billy Frank thought of baseball. He loved baseball. Among his favorite players were Babe Ruth, Joe DiMaggio, and Mel Ott. Billy Frank's most favorite player was Lou Gehrig of the New York Yankees. Gehrig had won the Triple Crown batting title in 1934, and his picture had appeared on the back of the Wheaties box. Billy Frank had bought his own box and carefully cut out the picture, which he carried inside his composition book. Did that constitute idolatry? Billy Frank knew for certain that he was much more enthusiastic about listening to a rousing game of baseball on the crystal radio set than about going to church or reading his Bible.

After several weeks, in early November, just before his sixteenth birthday, Billy Frank could no longer stand it. He had listened to enough of Mordecai Ham's preaching by now to know that he "wasn't right with God," as the preacher put it. He did not have a two-way relationship with the God of the

Bible, and as Dr. Ham said, "God does not have any grandchildren. When they get to the pearly gates, no one will be able to get in because their mother or their father or their pastor or anyone else believed. The Bible says it is by faith you are saved. You, each of you, must individually invite Jesus Christ into your life to change you, to use you to do His work on earth."

Billy Frank stood straight and tall as he mouthed the words of the closing hymn, "Almost Persuaded, Now to Believe."

> Almost persuaded, come, come today;
> Almost persuaded, turn not away;
> Jesus invites you here,
> Angels are lingering near.

By the second verse of the hymn, Billy Frank could feel his heart beating fast. He wondered what would happen if he became a Christian. *Will my friends stick with me, or will I seem really strange to them? Do I really want to hand over my dreams, my future to God? What if He asks me to be a missionary or something worse?* Even though Billy Frank could think of a hundred reasons not to go forward as the hymn was being sung, by the third verse he put down his hymnal and began walking toward the front of the tabernacle.

> Almost persuaded, harvest is past!
> Almost persuaded, doom comes at last!

Billy Frank felt like his shoes were made of lead as he strode down the sawdust-covered aisle. Other people—men, women, boys, and girls—joined him. Just as the hymn ended, Billy Frank found himself in front of the platform. The woman beside him was weeping. Billy Frank's heart sank. He didn't feel like crying. In fact, he didn't feel anything much. *Am I really being saved?* he asked himself. *Or am I just making a fool of myself?* He thought about turning around and walking back to his seat, but he stayed put. Soon a family friend, J. D. Prevatt, stepped up beside him and put his arm around Billy Frank. "Are you here to make a decision for Christ?" he asked.

Billy Frank nodded.

"Praise God," JD said. "Do you understand that God wants you to turn from your sin and ask Jesus Christ into your life?"

Again, Billy Frank nodded, slowly and clearly. JD went on to explain the gospel and prayed with him. Although there were no tears, Billy Frank knew that something had changed in him that night. For the first time in weeks he felt peaceful. He wanted to read his Bible even when no one was watching, and he carried a small hymnal with him. (He read rather than sang the hymns, though.) He told his parents what had happened to him, and they were overjoyed. Billy Frank also wanted to mark his conversion in a special way and decided to drop the Frank part of his name. From now on he would be called Billy Graham. He thought it sounded much more dignified.

When he told his school friends that he was now a Christian with a new name, many of them took to calling him Preacher Boy instead of Billy. Some of them were no longer eager to spend time with him, but new friends soon replaced them. One of Billy's new friends was Grady Wilson, the boy he had stood beside in the choir at Dr. Ham's meetings. Grady and his older brother, Thomas Walter, whom everyone knew as TW, had both gone forward to receive Christ the night after Billy had. They also were now trying to live Christian lives. Billy and Grady often talked about what God wanted them to do once they left school in a year and a half, but neither of them knew what it might be.

The following year another traveling evangelist passed through the area and stayed at the Graham house. His name was Jimmie Johnson, and he was very different from Mordecai Ham. Jimmie was young, athletic, and handsome. He looked and sounded like a movie star, with flashing brown eyes, dark hair, and an Alabama drawl. Jimmie had graduated from Bob Jones College in Cleveland, Tennessee, and was on a preaching circuit of the South. While Jimmie stayed at the Graham home, Billy followed him around as much as he could. One day they went to the jail in Monroe, North Carolina, where Jimmie preached to the inmates. Jimmie was midway through his sermon when he suddenly looked over at Billy. "Now," he said, pointing straight at him, "here's a fellow who knows what it means to be saved. He's gonna tell you what Jesus Christ has done in his life."

Sixteen-year-old Billy Graham stumbled to his feet, unsure about what he could say to the men. His opening line was awkward and inappropriate:

"I'm glad to see so many of you out and about this afternoon." The words were already out of his mouth before he realized he was talking to jailed men. Feeling embarrassed, he started again. This time Billy followed the style of testimony he'd heard at big evangelical rallies. "I was a sinner," he said, "and a no-good. I didn't care anything about God, the Bible, or people." He went on to say, "Jesus changed my life. He gave me peace and joy. He can give you peace and joy. He will forgive your sins as He forgave mine if you will only let Him into your heart." As he spoke, Billy twisted the hem of his coat so many times that it looked like a rope.

Billy then sat down and promised himself he would never do that again. It was nerve-wracking to speak in front of people. He would leave that to Grady Wilson, who was becoming quite a good preacher. Since Grady didn't have a car, Billy often drove him to various places to preach.

All of this activity, though, plus getting up at 2:30 every morning to milk cows, cut into Billy's ability to concentrate at school. In fact, at Christmas 1935, the semester before Billy was due to graduate, Billy's teacher visited Mrs. Graham. She told her that Billy often fell asleep in her eleven o'clock English class. Still, there wasn't much anyone could do about the situation. Billy prayed that he would scrape through and graduate with the other twenty-four members of the senior class. Somehow he managed to do so, walking proudly across the stage at commencement.

Now that he had graduated from high school, the question became what to do next. His mother wanted him to go to Wheaton College in Illinois, but

Billy seriously doubted that his grades were good enough or that he would enjoy studying as hard as he would have to at a college like Wheaton. Grady's brother, TW, was already studying at Bob Jones College, and Grady was eager to join him there. Billy thought back to his time with Jimmie Johnson, who was a graduate of Bob Jones College. Jimmie was an excellent preacher, and he was confident and relaxed, two things Billy aspired to be one day. *Perhaps going to Bob Jones College would turn me into a man like Jimmie,* he told himself.

Billy quickly sent off an application to Bob Jones College. This left him with the question of what to do over the summer. The Grahams were better off financially than most of their neighbors and would be able to help Billy with his tuition costs, but he would still need spending money. The answer turned out to be something Billy had never considered—selling products door-to-door for the Fuller Brush Company.

Albert McMakin, Billy's old friend, was now sales manager for the Fuller Brush Company in South Carolina, and he offered Billy summer work. Billy was reluctant at first, but Albert assured him he could make good money. Albert said it was fun and easy. All Billy had to do was knock on strangers' doors and try to get them to buy something. That didn't sound like fun to Billy. In fact, it sounded downright scary.

Chapter 3

Griping Not Tolerated!

Seventeen-year-old Billy Graham, his official Fuller Brush suitcase in hand, took a deep breath before walking up the path to the front door of the house. He was ready for action. He had pored over the red and white catalog until he knew all of the two hundred brushes offered by the company, and their uses. Now it was time to try his hand at selling them. He knocked on the door, and a middle-aged woman answered. "Hello, Ma'am," he said, tipping his hat. "I'm here representing the Fuller Brush Company, and I have a free gift for you. Would you prefer a pastry brush or a vegetable brush?"

The woman smiled. "Thank you, young man. I believe I'll have the pastry brush." With that the woman snatched the brush out of his hand. "And good day," she said as she shut the door firmly.

Billy didn't move. He hadn't even had the opportunity to launch into his sales banter. Not only that, the woman had cost him ten cents, since the cost of the introductory gift came out of his pocket. He knocked on the door again, but no one answered. As Billy walked back down to the street, he realized that he would have to change his sales approach if he wanted to earn any money.

Over the next few weeks Billy worked hard at sharpening his selling technique. First, he made sure that he got his foot in the door. As soon as someone opened the door, he put his foot inside so that the person could not shut it on him. Then he learned that it was much better to keep the gift at the bottom of the suitcase. That way, for a housewife to receive the free brush, Billy would have to be invited in to unpack his case. He was hopeful that the woman of the house would become interested in the other brushes as he laid them out on the table.

Billy also learned to read clues. Sometimes he felt like a junior detective. If he saw a bowl of dog food in the corner, he would ask the woman if she needed a dog brush. If he spotted a man's coat hanging on a hook, perhaps her husband needed a clothes brush. And if he heard a refrigerator humming in the kitchen, he would point out that the expensive, modern appliance would last much longer if the coils on the back were cleaned with a Fuller Brush once a week.

Billy worked hard selling brushes. At night he stayed with Albert in cheap boardinghouses all over North and South Carolina. The two of them managed to get by on a dollar a day, eating their meals with other traveling salesmen and a few drifters. The highlight of Billy's day was gathering in the living room with the other guests to listen to radio coverage of the 1936 Olympic Games in Berlin, Germany. It was thrilling to follow the exploits of Jesse Owens as he won medal after medal for the United States team.

Even with the thrill of the Olympic Games, it was not long before Billy became homesick. He'd been away from home before—to the Magnolia Gardens in Charleston, South Carolina, and as far as Tahlequah, Oklahoma, where his uncle Tom had married a Cherokee woman. But on those occasions he had traveled with his family. He had never been away from home on his own for an extended period of time. Even with Albert around in the evenings, he was lonely.

On more than one occasion Billy thought about packing up and heading home, until he struck on an idea. He asked Albert if Grady and TW could join them on the job. Albert agreed, and soon Billy had his friends with him. It made all the difference. The three friends loved to play practical jokes on each other, but they also had a serious side. Every night they would pray and read the Bible together in their boarding-house rooms. Many of the families they visited while selling brushes during the day also got to hear the young men tell about their Christian faith. Each week as Billy did this, he gained confidence in speaking to strangers, and his sales increased. It wasn't long before he was earning seventy-five dollars a week, a small fortune for a boy just out of high school.

By the end of summer Billy was excited about attending Bob Jones College. He knew for sure that he did not want to be a Fuller Brush man for the rest of his life. As fall rolled around, Billy and the Wilson brothers returned home, where they spent a week with their families before heading off to college.

On a bright September day Billy and his father loaded up the old Plymouth, collected the Wilson brothers, and headed west across the Appalachians to Cleveland, Tennessee. They pulled up at Bob Jones College, which was dominated by a two-story, red-brick building with white colonnades and a large veranda. "We call that Old Main," TW informed them. "You're going to love it here."

An hour later, Billy wasn't so sure. He walked into his dorm room with its two sets of bunks and was greeted with a sign that read, "Griping Not Tolerated!" He stared at the sign. It seemed so out of place at a Christian college. He wondered why arriving students weren't being welcomed with a Bible verse instead of this sign.

Within a week, Billy realized that there was a lot to gripe about. His parents had always expected good behavior from their children, but nothing like what Bob Jones College required. The list of rules went on and on. The young men and women were allowed to date, but only if they had an older chaperone with them the entire time. Even then they were not allowed to sit together on a sofa. Dates had to be preapproved by the faculty, and outside of their official date, couples were not allowed to talk to each other. There were rules about classes, too. It seemed to Billy that many of these rules weren't about encouraging thinking through or debating the various sides of an issue. Billy and his three roommates discussed their concerns in whispers after the lights were out. That way they couldn't see the "Griping Not Tolerated!" sign.

One of Billy's roommates, Wendell Phillips, decided he could not take the strict routine any longer and left the college one morning without warning. Later he sent Billy a letter from a Bible college in Florida, telling him that he liked his new college a lot better. Billy was thinking about leaving Bob Jones College himself when he and Grady both came down with a serious case of the flu. They were sent to the school infirmary, where they were expected to lie flat on their backs and stare at the ceiling. Billy soon got bored with this and had someone smuggle a movie projector and a copy of a Mickey Mouse film into the infirmary. When it was discovered he'd screened a movie in the infirmary, Billy was given one hundred demerit points. Not watching movies was another rule.

The college discipline system had a rule that a student with 150 demerit points was automatically expelled. Billy was getting close to that number. Although he wanted to leave Bob Jones College, he didn't want it to be through expulsion. He kept his head down until the end of the first semester, when he was glad to head home to North Carolina for Christmas.

Over the holidays the Graham family took a road trip to Orlando, Florida, to visit Billy's aunt and uncle, who had purchased a boardinghouse in the sleepy town. Billy enjoyed being with his family again. It seemed as if everyone had grown since he'd left, even little Jean, now four years old. Jean asked Billy a thousand questions as they drove south.

Billy loved everything about Orlando: the endless rows of orange trees on the edge of town; the warm, dry winter weather; and the swimming holes. While they were in the central Florida area, Billy convinced his parents to let him visit his old roommate, Wendell Phillips, at the Florida Bible Institute in Temple Terrace, near Tampa, about seventy miles away.

As soon as Billy walked onto the campus, he felt at home. The Florida Bible Institute was housed in a Spanish-style former hotel complex that had gone bankrupt during the financial crash of 1929. The stucco buildings were painted pink, and the property had an eighteen-hole golf course that stretched in a crescent shape around the hotel buildings and along the bank of the Hillsborough River. The whole atmosphere was relaxed, like a large family living together. Right away Billy knew that the Florida Bible Institute was where he wanted to be. However, since his parents had paid for another semester at Bob Jones College, he felt he should return there.

As Christmas vacation ended, Billy realized just how much he dreaded going back to Cleveland. Billy talked to his parents about the situation, and they agreed that he might be better suited for the Florida Bible Institute. His mother was particularly worried about his recurring cough and liked the idea of her son living in a warmer climate.

Driving over the Appalachians once again to Tennessee, Billy knew he had to find the courage to talk to Dr. Bob Jones. Back at the college in Cleveland, he chewed his fingernails down to the quick as he waited outside the president's office. Eventually the secretary waved him into Dr. Jones's office.

"What is it?" Bob Jones said when Billy entered his office. "I've been hearing things about you."

Billy opened his mouth to speak, but nothing came out. He tried again. Slowly, he managed to tell the president that he didn't like the college—that he felt out of place and far from God.

Deep in his heart, Billy knew that his time at Bob Jones College was over. He did not want to stay one day longer than he had to. By mid-January Billy had been accepted to the Florida Bible Institute, and his father arrived to pick him up from Bob Jones College. He felt better with every mile that his father's new 1937 Plymouth took him away from Cleveland, Tennessee.

As they drove along, Billy imagined what campus life would be like at the Florida Bible Institute in Temple Terrace. No more cold, damp classrooms, no more strict rules, and no more anti-griping posters. It was going to be wonderful.

As it turned out, it was. The Florida Bible Institute had just seventy students enrolled, thirty men and forty women. Students had plenty of time to study, work, and have fun. Most of the campus was not used for students, so the extra rooms were rented out during the winter to Christians from the north who wanted to get away from the snow and ice. About fifty guests stayed all winter, and church groups came for shorter lengths of time. The students were paid twenty cents an hour to run the guest facilities. Billy did not need extra money. His father had happily paid the dollar-a-day college fees and provided him with pocket money. Billy, however, wanted to enter fully into college life and took his turn waiting tables, washing dishes, and mowing the lawn. Soon he found a job that he loved so much—caddying on the golf course—that he didn't care whether or not he got paid for it.

Walking long distances on the course while carrying a heavy set of golf clubs helped Billy use up some of his energy, but it was the men Billy caddied for who made the job fascinating and enjoyable. Some of the guests were aging, well-known evangelists, and Billy could hardly believe that he had them all to himself for eighteen holes of golf. He got to know Gipsy Smith, William Evans of the Moody Bible Institute, and W. B. Riley, founder and president of Northwestern Schools. As they walked from hole to hole, Billy got to ask questions and even try out some of his sermons on them. This was a good thing, because the school required all its students to preach at various sites around the community, including trailer parks, jails, street corners, churches, and youth groups. Billy was regularly assigned to speak at The Stockade, Tampa's jail, and at nearby Tin Can Trailer Park.

Although he was still gangly and shy, Billy wanted to improve his preaching ability and worked hard at doing so. He often paddled a canoe across the

Hillsborough River to a small island populated with alligators and white herons. He would belt out his sermons, repeating them over and over until they felt natural. Then he would add gestures to emphasize the important points. When he paddled back across the river, his fellow students would tease him, "How many converts did you get today, Billy?"

As Billy progressed through the Florida Bible Institute, he began to win some converts to the Christian faith. Most of them were from Tin Can Trailer Park, where he was a regular fixture. Two women organized open-air church services there, which attracted between two hundred and one thousand people. Billy soon realized how effective it was to incorporate current events into his sermons. Ordinary people were drawn to stories about what was going on in the world and what the Bible had to say about it. Billy had a lot to talk about. In September 1939, Germany invaded Poland, and World War II began in Europe. In Asia, the Japanese seized control of large swaths of eastern China. President Franklin D. Roosevelt assured Americans that if war broke out, the United States would remain neutral. Despite the president's assurances, the American people were worried about what might happen next.

When his second year of Bible school was over, Billy decided to stay in Temple Terrace instead of going home. He wanted to keep preaching over the summer, and that was what he did. Sometimes he preached on the streets of Tampa seven times a day as well as preaching at youth services and churches. Many of the churches that opened their pulpits to

Billy were from the Southern Baptist denomination. Over time, the fact that Billy had been baptized as a baby in the Presbyterian church rather than by full immersion as an adult became an issue. Billy's mentor, Cecil Underwood, suggested that Billy consider being baptized in the Baptist tradition, to which Billy agreed. Soon afterward Cecil suggested Billy become an ordained Baptist minister. This, too, was arranged, and at age twenty-one, Billy Graham became an ordained Southern Baptist minister.

Billy was now able to perform weddings and funerals and take on more preaching roles. However, he had bigger plans. The Florida Bible Institute was a great school, but it was not accredited, which meant other colleges and universities did not recognize its degrees. With graduation looming, Billy realized that he wanted an accredited degree. He wasn't sure how this would work out, since his grade point average at high school was so low. The problem was solved when two men came to stay at the campus in Temple Terrace. One of the men was Paul Fischer, an attorney from Chicago. The other was a Chicago businessman named Elner Edman. Elner's uncle was the chairman of the board of Wheaton College, just outside Chicago, and his brother Ray was a professor there. Both men heard Billy preach and were so impressed that they offered to write letters of recommendation to Wheaton urging the school to accept Billy as a student. Better yet, they offered to pay his tuition and expenses if he was accepted. It was more than Billy could have dreamed of.

In May 1940, when Billy graduated from the Florida Bible Institute, he had his acceptance for Wheaton College in his hand. He spent the summer preaching in Pennsylvania before heading west to Chicago.

Chapter 4

The Girl of His Dreams

It was a clear fall morning in 1940 when Billy Graham arrived on the Wheaton College campus, twenty-five miles west of Chicago. The campus was an inspiring sight, with its impressive red-brick buildings and stately rows of oak trees. Wheaton had a long and prestigious history. It had been founded eighty years before by a staunch antislavery Congregational minister named Jonathan Blanchard and had developed into a well-respected and fully accredited liberal arts and science institution. Yet it had not lost its Christian roots—far from it. Every student studied the Bible throughout his or her time at the college, and all of the faculty members were active Christians.

Billy anticipated a smooth transition to Wheaton, but upon his arrival, he felt hopelessly out of place.

At nearly twenty-two years of age he was the oldest and, he believed, the oddest-looking freshman. He was six feet two inches tall, weighed about 160 pounds, and covered his gaunt frame with brightly colored clothes that had been fine in Florida but looked unusual among the preppy northern students. When Billy tried to talk, the other students seemed startled by his strong Southern drawl. Some told him that they couldn't understand a word he was saying. While many of the freshmen students came from top high schools and preparatory schools in the North and East, in his heart, Billy was still a farm boy from North Carolina.

By the time Billy had stowed his few belongings in his room, he felt a sense of gloom settle over him. How was he going to make it through three and a half years of study at Wheaton? (His credits from the Florida Bible Institute allowed him to skip his first semester at the college.) To make matters worse, Wheaton College had just about as many rules as Bob Jones College. These included no dancing, no playing cards, no joining secret societies, and no tobacco or alcohol in any form.

Although Billy had enrolled at Wheaton to pursue becoming an evangelist, he decided to major in anthropology—the study of human beings and their cultures. He felt this would help him understand people from all over the world. If he did happen to go to foreign countries as a missionary or preacher, he hoped to have a better idea of the people there and how best to reach them with the gospel. Besides studying anthropology, Billy took classes in New Testament Greek, geology, and economics. All in all, it involved a lot of study.

Billy slowly began to feel like he belonged at Wheaton. On Sunday mornings he visited one of his professors, Mortimer Lane. Dr. Lane and his family belonged to the Plymouth Brethren denomination. They hosted a small group of Brethren and others interested in prayer, worship, and Bible study in their home. Billy was glad to have somewhere to go. He felt at home with the Lane family.

Located about a mile from the college campus was an auditorium, where on Sundays about three hundred people gathered for a church service. The church was officially called the United Gospel Tabernacle, but everyone simply referred to it as "the Tab." Billy was soon routinely invited to preach at the Tab, for which he was paid an honorarium of fifteen dollars. Again, Billy often used current events to illustrate his sermons. The war in Europe was always a stirring topic. By June 1940 the German army had overrun Paris, and Italy had declared war against France and the United Kingdom. Still, the European conflict seemed a long way away.

While the fifteen-dollar honorarium Billy received when he preached at the Tab was helpful, he needed to earn more pocket money. To do this he teamed up with a student named Johnny Streater. Johnny had an ancient yellow Ford pickup truck, which he used to haul furniture for people in the neighboring towns around Wheaton. He offered Billy a job working each afternoon for fifty cents an hour, twice the newly mandated minimum wage. Billy soon learned his way around the west side of Chicago.

One day in November 1940, Billy and Johnny were hanging out around Williston Hall, the girls' dorm, when Johnny yelled, "Hey, Ruth. Over here!" Billy watched as a slim brunette with long pig-tails walked down the stairs. "Hi, Johnny," she said in an accent Billy could not quite place. Johnny grinned. "Billy, this is the girl I've been telling you about, Ruth Bell." Billy felt his face growing red. He stammered some kind of greeting and stepped back. He remembered Johnny telling him about Ruth. He said she was the prettiest junior in the school, and one of the most devout too. While Billy didn't know how devout Ruth was, he had to agree that she was probably the prettiest girl in school. Soon afterward Billy and Johnny were bumping along on their way to Glen Ellyn to pick up a couch. As they drove, Billy could not stop thinking about Ruth.

Back at Wheaton, Billy began asking around to find out all he could about Ruth. She was the younger daughter of Dr. Nelson Bell and his wife, Virginia. The Bells were medical missionaries in China, and Ruth had lived her whole life in Asia, first with her parents and older sister Rosa in Tsing-kiang, three hundred miles northwest of Shanghai, and then in a Christian boarding school at Pyong-yang in northern Korea. Ruth had followed her sister Rosa to Wheaton, while her parents, along with two younger siblings, Clayton and Virginia, remained in China.

Ruth's background intrigued Billy, as did her reputation for disciplined Christian living. This included waking at the crack of dawn to read and pray before breakfast. A month after their first encounter, Billy found himself in the library at Blanchard Hall, where Ruth was studying. Billy's friend Howard Van Buren kicked him under the table. "Go on, Billy. Ask her to the concert," he whispered. "You know you want to. Just get up and do it."

Billy sat for a long time hunched over his books before he stood up and walked over to Ruth. The librarian glared at him as he mumbled, "Hey Ruth, could I take you to the concert next Sunday afternoon?"

Ruth's hazel eyes twinkled as she nodded. "Sure, I'd love to go." These were the best words Billy had heard in a long time.

The following Sunday Billy and Ruth went to hear Handel's *Messiah* performed. The music was wonderful, but Billy hardly heard it. His attention was glued to the girl he was with. Billy liked everything about her: the way she talked, the way she laughed, the way she cocked her head when she listened to the music.

That night Billy wrote to his mother. "I have just met a wonderful girl. Her name is Ruth Bell. She looks a little like you, and even her voice sounds like you. This is the girl I am going to marry."

The path of true love did not go smoothly for Billy, however. This was partly because he had fallen in love with a young woman whose lifelong goal had been to be a single female missionary in

Tibet. Wooing her was not easy, and although Ruth was happy to date Billy, she told him she could not imagine being his wife. Before long Billy realized it was impossible to change Ruth's heart on his own, and he started praying that God would take charge of their relationship.

In March 1941 Ruth's sister Rosa was diagnosed with tuberculosis and confined to her bed. Ruth dropped out of school to move home and look after her. Summer was looming on the horizon, and Billy was planning to head down to Florida to conduct some evangelistic meetings. Before he left, he asked Ruth to marry him, but she would not give him a straight answer. As Billy packed the Plymouth and drove south from Wheaton, his heart was heavy. He hoped he had not put Ruth off entirely with his last words to her. "I think it would be a very good idea if you would forget your girlhood ideals, your crazy ideas, and the advice of your friends. Forget it all. And just be Ruth Bell for a while," he had said.

Billy arrived safely in Florida and set up "base camp" at the Florida Bible Institute in Temple Terrace. It was good to see his old professors again, and the warm air blowing in off the Gulf of Mexico invigorated him and his preaching. Billy was grateful when letters began arriving from Ruth. She wrote about her daily routines, how Rosa was doing, and how she was enjoying visiting with her parents. The situation in China under Japanese occupation had deteriorated so much that it was no longer safe for Western missionaries to remain in the country, and reluctantly Dr. Bell had left his medical work in China and returned with his family to the United States.

On July 6, 1941, Billy received another letter from Ruth. As usual he rushed to his room to open it in private. Billy's heart nearly burst as he read, "I will marry you!" That night Billy preached up a storm at a local church, though in truth his thoughts were on Ruth and the life they would have together. When the sermon was over, Billy sat down beside the pastor.

"Do you know what you just said?" the pastor leaned over and asked.

"No," Billy replied honestly.

"I'm not sure anyone here does either!" the pastor remarked.

Billy grinned. He was too happy to let anything bother him.

In mid-July, Billy headed to Charlotte, North Carolina, to preach in a series of revival meetings at Sharon Presbyterian Church. When the meetings were over, the church took up an offering for him. It came to $165, and there was only one thing Billy wanted to buy with the money—an engagement ring. With the ring in hand, he headed west to Black Mountain, North Carolina, where Ruth was staying in a cabin with some friends from China. High on a mountaintop, Billy presented the engagement ring to Ruth, who told him she would have to get permission from her parents before she wore it. The next day she sent a telegram to her parents in Virginia asking, "Billy has offered me a ring. May I wear it?"

The response from her parents arrived quickly. "Yes, if it fits."

Ruth put on the ring, and she and Billy began planning their wedding, which would take place in two years' time, after they graduated from Wheaton College.

As the summer of 1941 drew to a close, Billy finally got the opportunity to meet Ruth's parents. He drove to Waynesboro, Virginia, to visit them, and he felt an instant bond with Dr. Bell and his wife. He could not believe how blessed he was to have them as his future in-laws.

Billy returned to Wheaton College with a spring in his step. Everything was going his way. He had the girl of his dreams, and he was on target to graduate on time. At this time the war in Europe and the Japanese aggression in Asia and the eastern Pacific region dominated much of the news. Then on the evening of December 7, 1941, someone at the Tab told Billy that the Japanese had attacked Pearl Harbor. Billy did not know where that was, but on the way home from the church service, he saw a newsboy selling a special edition of the *Chicago Tribune*. The headline on the front page read, "US at War with Japan."

A short while later Billy was at the Lanes' house, glued to the radio, learning the grim details of the assault that had taken place. At 7:55 a.m. in Hawaii, Japanese fighter planes attacked Pearl Harbor, sinking or damaging twenty-one naval vessels that were part of the US Pacific Fleet docked there, and killing 2,402 servicemen. The following day the United States officially declared war on Japan. Three days later, on December 11, 1941, the United States declared war on Germany and Italy in response to their declaration of war against America.

Now that the country was at war, Billy's immediate response was to sign up for the military. He knew the army would need chaplains, and he wrote to the War Department offering his services. He soon received a letter back telling him he had two choices if he wanted to be an army chaplain. He could either finish his degree and take a seminary course before applying to become a chaplain, or he could serve as a pastor for a year and then attend chaplaincy training at Harvard University. Billy was pleased to get started.

Chapter 5

Seeing the Possibilities

On a warm spring day in 1943 a large black Lincoln Continental pulled up in front of the house where Billy Graham rented a room. Billy watched from his bedroom window on the second floor as a curly-haired man wearing a bow tie got out of the car and bounded up the front steps. A minute later Billy's landlady knocked on his door. "There's a man here to see you. He says his name is Bob Van Kampen."

Billy followed the landlady downstairs. He couldn't remember ever hearing that name before, and he wondered how Bob had found his address. The two men shook hands in the living room, and Bob got straight to the point. "I'm a deacon at the Western Springs Baptist Church. I don't know if you remember me."

Billy thought hard for a moment. He recalled a couple of preaching assignments at the small church held in a basement about twelve miles southeast of Wheaton. "Yes, yes, I remember," Billy replied. "What can I do for you?"

Bob smiled. "We need a new pastor. Our church board was impressed with your preaching and would like to offer you the job. I understand you will be graduating this year."

"Yes," Billy said. "And I'm getting married soon after. Would that be a problem?"

"Not at all," Bob said. "There's plenty of work to keep a married couple busy. We have about one hundred members, but only about fifty show up on any given Sunday. There's plenty to do convincing folks to come back to church."

Billy nodded. He liked Bob's direct style.

"You'll be wanting to know about the money," Bob continued. "We can pay forty-five dollars a week and a dollar and a half for your phone, and can offer you a free furnished apartment. If the church pays the rent, then that won't be taxed. Why don't you and your fiancée come out to visit next weekend and see what you think?"

"That's a good idea," Billy said, "But you need to know that with the war on, I'm hoping to do one year as a pastor and then go to chaplaincy school at Harvard. How would you feel about a one-year appointment?"

Bob raised his hands. "Nothing is certain with the war on, is it? We'll pray that it's over by then, but it's hard to get a pastor, even for a year. We'd be glad if you'd come and get started."

The following Sunday Billy and Ruth attended Western Springs Baptist Church. Services were held in the basement of what would eventually be the sanctuary, and the church was raising money to complete the building. Billy preached, and the congregation warmly received him and Ruth.

Following the service, Billy and Bob spent more time talking together. Billy learned that the deacon was the president of Hitchcock Publishing Company in Chicago and the treasurer of the National Gideon Association that put Bibles in hotel rooms across America.

The next month Billy visited Bob and agreed to take on the pastorate at Western Springs Baptist Church. However, he forgot to consult Ruth before making the decision, and Ruth was furious when she learned he'd made the arrangement. "It's not so much that you accepted the call, Billy. It's that you never even thought about how it would affect me. You have to think about both of us now. If I'm going to be your wife, then I am your partner, too," she told him.

Billy felt confused. His father had done all the leading in his house, and his mother had done the following. It appeared that things were done differently in the Bell household. Ruth assumed she would have a say in whatever happened to them as a couple. Billy apologized to his fiancée and promised to do his best in the future, but he knew that making decisions on his own would be a hard pattern to break.

In June both Billy and Ruth graduated from Wheaton College. Two months later, on the evening of Friday, August 13, 1943, they were married in the Presbyterian church in Montreat, North Carolina, where Ruth's parents now lived. (Ruth had told Billy before their wedding that she had no intention of leaving behind her Presbyterian roots to become a Baptist like him.) Following their wedding they honeymooned in the Blue Ridge Mountains, staying in private homes that rented rooms for a dollar a night and eating in local diners. It didn't matter that they did not have much money. Billy and Ruth were glad to finally be starting married life together.

Following the honeymoon they headed back to Chicago, where the church had rented them an upstairs apartment in Hinsdale, a suburb neighboring Western Springs. It took them only two hours to unpack all their belongings in their new home. The fifty active members of the church gave the Grahams a warm welcome, complete with a bouquet of two dozen roses, some fresh produce, an offering of forty-eight dollars, and a wedding cake.

Billy and Ruth threw themselves into church work. Billy spent hours preparing sermons while Ruth scoured old copies of *Reader's Digest* and various newspapers, looking for illustrations that Billy could use. Billy preached twice on Sunday, ran a midweek prayer meeting, and taught child evangelism classes with Ruth on Wednesday afternoons. In addition, Billy and Ruth visited every family that came into contact with the church. Their efforts began to pay off. Soon more people started attending church services each Sunday, and by Christmas one hundred people were regularly attending.

For a special evening out, Billy and Ruth loved to go into Chicago to watch newsreels at Telenews, a theater on North State Street. Of course, much of the news was about the war, and the couple would watch newsreels of American soldiers fighting the Germans in Europe and the Japanese in the Pacific.

For Christmas 1943, Billy and Ruth decided to stay in Hinsdale for one special reason. On January 2, 1944, Billy was to take over a radio program called *Songs in the Night*. Another pastor, Torrey Johnson, had been running the show, but it proved too much of a commitment for his church. So Torrey had sought out Billy and asked him if he would like to take it over. There was just one catch. It cost $150 a week to buy radio airtime from station WCFL in Chicago. Agreeing to take over the show was a huge decision for a young pastor to make, but Billy didn't look at his limitations. Instead, he saw the possibilities the broadcast presented. WCFL could be heard all across the Midwest and into the South and East as well.

When Billy had first presented the idea to the church deacons, they voted against it. Too much money was at stake, they said. The entire church budget, including Billy's salary, was only $180 a month. Committing to take over *Songs in the Night* would add another $600 to it. Many in the congregation could not imagine where that kind of money would come from, especially since they were still raising money to complete the sanctuary. But like Billy, Bob could see the possibilities that a radio program broadcast directly from the church offered, so he decided to provide the necessary funds to get the program running. He told the church, "We need to support Billy. God's given him a special gift. He's going to be another Billy Sunday or Dwight L. Moody." That was all Billy needed to hear. He asked the Wheaton College Women's Glee Club to come to the church each Sunday night to sing backup. But what he still needed was a star attraction singer to put the program on the map.

As Billy prayed and thought about this person, one name came to mind—George Beverly Shea. Bev, as most people called him, was a powerful young baritone and an announcer at Moody Bible Institute's radio station. Billy realized that Bev would give *Songs in the Night* just what it needed, a name people recognized. The problem became how to get the singer to agree to come on the program.

Billy always preferred communicating directly, and early in December he set out for Chicago's North Side. As he drove, he rehearsed his speech. Billy felt a lot was riding on getting George Beverly Shea to join him on the radio show. He turned onto North LaSalle Street and stopped in front of Moody Bible Institute. He had been told the radio studio was on the top floor of the main building.

After climbing the steps to the top floor two at a time, Billy spied Bev through a glass door. The secretary explained that Bev was busy in a meeting and informed Billy that he would have to make an appointment and come back later. But Billy set to work using his best Fuller Brush salesman skills to keep the secretary talking until the office door opened. Then he sprang into action, rushing past the secretary and right into Bev's path.

"Mr. Shea," he began. "I'm sorry to bother you, but I have a quick question for you."

"Yes," Bev said, looking a little bemused.

Billy went on. "My name is Billy Graham, and I'm the pastor at the Western Springs Baptist Church . . ."

Bev Shea thrust out his hand to shake Billy's. "Yes, I've heard of you," he said.

Billy shook Bev's hand and plowed right on with his prepared speech about how Torrey Johnson had offered him the chance to take over *Songs in the Night* and how he desperately needed a marquee name like George Beverly Shea to give the show some star appeal. At first Bev was reluctant to agree, but Billy would not stop talking until Bev agreed to try it out for a few weeks. As Billy drove home, he was ecstatic. He still had much to do to make the radio show a success, but he was sure that having George Beverly Shea on board would make all the difference.

Ruth was as excited as Billy about the turn of events, and the two of them began writing scripts for the show. They soon discovered that filling in forty-five minutes of airtime took some effort. Billy would think of a popular topic, and Ruth would come up with some relevant stories or newspaper cuttings about it. Then they would handwrite a script, since they didn't have access to a typewriter. Billy had to write as neatly as he could so that he could read what he had written when he was on the air. Once they had a script for the show, they matched up songs that went along with the theme. The show would alternate three-minute talking segments with songs until the time was up.

On Sunday evening, January 2, 1944, *Songs in the Night* was broadcast live from the Village Church at Western Springs, as the Western Springs Baptist Church was now being called. Bev Shea was there to sing, but no one had advertised the fact, since the church was bursting at the seams with 125 people seated inside. There was simply no room for any more people in the live audience.

Under Billy's leadership, the radio show was an instant success. Within weeks the church was drawing up plans to expand to accommodate the crowds who wanted to attend the live performance. Soon all kinds of people began sending donations, ranging from ten cents to fifty dollars. Sometimes the weekly donations were enough to cover the cost of getting the show on the air. The *Chicago Tribune* even sent out a reporter to write a story on *Songs in the Night*. Since the show was broadcast so widely, churches in neighboring states began inviting Billy to come and speak at evangelistic rallies. Billy accepted many of these invitations, which caused a lot of strain in his relationships with some members of the church who resented his being away on so many Sundays.

In May 1944 Billy received an invitation from Torrey Johnson to speak at a new venture that was being called Chicagoland Youth for Christ. This new group's goal was to reach the servicemen and young people who flooded into the Michigan Avenue area of downtown Chicago on Saturday nights. The plan was to hold evangelistic rallies in Orchestra Hall on

South Michigan Avenue, and Billy was invited to be the speaker.

On Saturday night, May 27, Billy stood on the platform at Orchestra Hall and looked out across the sea of young faces. The hall seated three thousand people and was almost full to capacity. It was the largest crowd Billy had ever preached to. Billy felt a little tense at first as he launched into his sermon, but he soon fell into a relaxed rhythm. Following the appeal at the end of the meeting, forty young people came forward to receive Christ.

Billy was overjoyed. In fact, he caught the vision that night of reaching thousands of young people at a time with the gospel. Invitations soon followed to speak at other evangelistic rallies in Indianapolis, Philadelphia, and Detroit. Billy accepted the invitations. For the first time ever, instead of driving, he flew to the various cities to speak.

Despite the success of the evangelistic rallies and his duties as pastor, Billy continued to focus on the men away fighting in the war. In August, much to his delight, he was accepted into the army chaplaincy training program. His joy soon turned to frustration, however, when he learned that he had flunked the army's medical exam—he was three pounds underweight. Billy promised to eat more and try again the following month to pass the medical.

Gaining three pounds should have been a simple enough task. All it required was eating more snacks and drinking a few more sodas. But a month later Billy was even thinner, and for good reason—he had contracted the mumps virus. At first everyone thought it was funny that a twenty-six-year-old man had caught a disease normally associated with children, but the amusement soon subsided. Billy's case of the mumps turned into orchitis, a potentially deadly complication. Billy burned up with fever, and a doctor visited him daily to monitor his care. One week went by, and then another and another. Billy lost even more weight, until he was down to only 130 pounds and looked like a skeleton. In November, it seemed that he was beginning to make a slow recovery.

Throughout Billy's illness, Peter Stam III, a missionary preparing to leave for Africa the following year, filled in as the host of *Songs in the Night.* On learning of his illness, one radio listener sent Billy a check for one hundred dollars. Billy and Ruth decided to use the money to escape the brutal Illinois winter and visit Florida. They left the church and radio program in good hands and headed south. Billy was still very weak when they arrived in Miami. The couple rented a room in a cheap hotel about a mile from the beach. Each day Ruth helped Billy walk down to the ocean, where he would sit in the warm sun and breathe in the salt air. Each day Billy got a little better.

After they had been in Miami for about a week, Billy discovered that Torrey Johnson and his family were staying three blocks away. Billy looked them up, and Torrey invited him to go fishing. As the two men sat casting their fishing lines from a boat into the deep-blue water, the conversation turned to the future. "You have to help me get Youth for Christ off the ground," Torrey said.

"What's that?" Billy asked, remembering preaching at the Chicagoland Youth for Christ rally before he became ill. "Isn't it already working well?"

Torrey shook his head. "Chicagoland Youth for Christ is only the beginning. I've since found out that youth rallies and organizations are popping up all over the country to help young men and women who are on leave from the service or have been discharged. They all need to hear the gospel," Torrey said, his eyes ablaze. "My plan is to unite all of these groups—from New York to San Francisco—into one big, interdenominational organization. We'll hold mass rallies in tents in every city in America. What do you say, Billy?"

"What is it you want me to do?" he asked.

"Come on over and be our first full-time employee," Torrey replied. "I think I can get my church to let me work half-time, and then I could spend the rest of the time raising money to open a Youth for Christ office. But we need a front man, someone to become our national organizer, or even bigger than that— our *international* organizer. I believe God wants to spread these youth meetings around the world."

Billy stared at the horizon as his fishing line bobbed in the ocean. Somewhere deep in his heart he felt something stir. This, he was one hundred percent sure, was exactly what he had been born to do.

Chapter 6

Youth for Christ

In February 1945, Billy Graham stood before a crowd of five thousand young people in the City Auditorium in Atlanta, Georgia. He was there to launch Youth for Christ (YFC). With him on stage were a chalk artist and a number of musicians, including a Salvation Army band. Several servicemen gave their testimonies, and Billy then preached to the crowd. So much had happened in the two months since Billy and Torrey had gone fishing together in Miami. Billy had talked over Torrey's request to become YFC's first full-time staff member with Ruth, and together they had agreed that it was their next step. After returning to Chicago, Billy resigned his Western Springs pastoral position. Now he was traveling the country, meeting with pastors to explain what Youth for Christ was and seeking their support, as well as preaching at YFC rallies.

Meanwhile, Allied troops in Europe were making big advances in pushing back German forces. Greece and Belgium had been liberated, and bombers were making regular runs over German cities, inflicting heavy damage. Everyone believed it would not be long before the Germans surrendered. In Asia and the Pacific, Allied advances against the Japanese were proving successful. It was only a matter of time before the Japanese would also surrender.

Soon hundreds of thousands of young American men, along with the women who had served in support roles and as nurses, would return home to the United States. Like Billy, some of these men and women came from rural settings, while others came from big cities. In the course of the war they had been transported to all sorts of places. Some had been sent to fight on remote islands in the middle of the Pacific Ocean, where the realties of war had had a deep impact on them. Billy knew that it was not going to be easy for many of these men and women to make the transition from fighting back to civilian life. Like Torrey, he believed that because of their experiences, these servicemen and women were going to be spiritually hungry. He was eager to see YFC established and running throughout the United States and Canada.

Organizing evangelistic rallies that would both entertain and challenge the listeners required a delicate balance. "We have to be careful," Torrey told Billy, "and pray that God gives us the sense not to use too much showmanship and the courage to use enough." This proved to be a challenge. Various rallies had included such things as show horses bowing before a wooden cross, four hundred nurses marching in the form of a cross, a former champion runner running a mile in front of the crowd, as well as magicians, ventriloquists, various soloists and singing groups—from duets to quartets to an entire orchestra performing—not to mention all manner of war heroes, famous people, and businessmen giving their testimonies. As far as Billy saw it, they needed to use whatever means necessary to engage the crowd and make each person present receptive to the preaching of the gospel.

As Billy kept busy traveling the country, YFC added a second evangelist, Charles Templeton, who was from Canada. Charles, or Chuck, as everyone called him, and Billy often toured together, and between them was a lot of showmanship. Billy wore blue suede shoes, while Chuck experimented with a bow tie that flashed with tiny red lights. Despite the entertainment factor, at every gathering the men were genuinely committed to preaching the gospel loudly and clearly. Both Billy and Chuck gave the same invitation, inviting anyone who wanted to become a Christian or to renew his or her commitment to Jesus Christ to come forward for prayer.

The model they followed was a simple one, but it worked well. Soon Billy and Chuck were drawing huge crowds. Requests poured in from around the country and Canada for evangelistic rallies and for help establishing YFC in various communities. Given all the travel this involved, Billy and Chuck were grateful when Walter Block, a YFC supporter, offered them the use of his United Airlines account. They could fly anywhere in the continental United States and Walter would pay for it. They took full use of the offer. Within the first year Billy clocked two hundred thousand air miles—more miles than anyone else in the country. That was aside from the countless hours he spent on Greyhound buses and trains, traveling to speak at rallies and church services in forty-seven states and every province in Canada. It was a big change for a country boy who until then had never seen the Pacific Ocean or crossed the Canadian border.

Other changes occurred. In early May 1945, Germany surrendered to the Allies. The war in Europe was over. And on September 2, the Japanese surrendered. Soon servicemen were flooding back to the United States. The biggest change of all, as far as Billy was concerned, was the news that Ruth was expecting a baby. Billy was delighted and thankful for this, since the doctor had told him that because of his orchitis he would probably never be a father. Now, in September, he was going to be one.

The news about the baby led to some serious thinking and praying for the Grahams. Billy and Ruth would be spending a lot of time apart—up to half the year. Ruth was no longer a pastor's wife. She was an evangelist's wife. It made sense for her to settle where she felt she had the most support for her and the baby. That place was an easy call to make. Ruth wanted to live with her parents in Montreat, North Carolina, where Billy could visit as often as possible. It was an unusual arrangement, but Billy knew Ruth would need help with the baby as well as a place to put down roots.

Billy and Ruth relocated to Montreat, and on September 21, 1945, Virginia Graham was born. Billy was preaching in Mobile, Alabama, at the time. He rushed home as soon as he could to see his new daughter, who had already acquired the nickname Gigi.

Youth For Christ was catching on quickly in the postwar era, and within a year over three hundred groups were spread across North America. Requests from farther afield poured in.

During March and April 1946, Billy, Chuck, Torrey, and Stratton Shufelt—the music director from Moody Church in Chicago—accompanied by Wesley Hartzell, a reporter for Hearst newspapers, set out for Great Britain and continental Europe to launch YFC there. Another man, Gavin Hamilton, had gone on ahead to set up meetings in Great Britain. It was Billy's first time overseas, and he had little idea of what to expect.

Things did not start out well. Traveling overseas in postwar conditions proved to be a wild adventure. The group set out from Chicago in an ex-military DC-4 airplane. The plane was still fitted with the hard bucket seats used to transport soldiers during the war. The group's route had them stopping in Toronto, Montreal, and then Gander, Newfoundland, to refuel. From there they would fly across the Atlantic Ocean, refuel in Shannon, Ireland, and land in London. But things went wrong as they approached Gander. By then it was late at night, and the town was engulfed in a heavy snowstorm. Soon the pilot announced that they would have to land at a small US Air Force base nearby.

The plane managed to land safely. Much to everyone's surprise, the Youth for Christ workers were hurried off the aircraft and asked to perform for the military men in a late-night impromptu concert. Billy surmised the base must have been short on entertainment, because the theater was filled with whistling and cheering men. Chuck strolled on stage and told a few stories to warm up the crowd. Billy peeked from behind the curtains. He could see that the crowd was getting restless. "Where are the girls?" someone yelled.

"Yes, we want to see girls!" another yelled.

Suddenly it dawned on Billy. Torrey had told the pilot when they left Chicago that they were an entertainment team. He guessed the pilot had supposed them to be a vaudeville act and had radioed ahead to the base commander, who then invited them to perform for the military men.

Stratton hurried onto the stage and sang a hymn. The crowd booed. Billy prayed hard. He was next up.

Billy walked onto the stage and waited for the booing to stop. Then he apologized for not being who the men thought they were, following up his apology with an explanation of who they were and why he was a Christian. That did not go well either. The base commander stepped in and stopped the show. Backstage, with the veins in his neck pulsating, he told the group of Christian men, "I should throw you in jail for misleading me like that. No one wants to come out in the middle of the night to hear a bunch of middle-aged men talk about Jesus!"

The next morning, Billy and the other men were grateful to be allowed back onto the airplane. However, their trials were not yet over. They made it safely to Shannon for refueling but ran into more heavy snow as they approached London. The aircraft was not allowed to land and was instead diverted to Edinburgh, Scotland. When the plane finally landed, the group rushed to the railway station and caught the train south to London. The meeting with a large group of pastors was already under way when the visitors from North America stumbled into the church.

Billy was the featured speaker, and as he walked onto the stage he took a deep breath. He had never preached to an English crowd and wondered how they would respond. He soon found out. They did not laugh at the same jokes as his American audiences did, nor did they find the same current events he used as illustrations engaging. Still, Billy made it through the evening and was glad when he was done.

The next morning Billy's host drove him around London. Billy was astounded by the damage German bombers had inflicted on the city. A number of buildings were nothing more than bombed-out hulks, while others had collapsed into piles of rubble that were slowly being cleared away.

Bit by bit Billy adjusted to the different ways the British said and did things. He also got used to the ever-present cup of tea, which he began to prefer over coffee. Like many other food items in England following the war, coffee was rationed and in short supply. To make it go farther, the coffee was mixed with chicory, and Billy soon decided that the beverage was more chicory than coffee. Fresh eggs were nearly nonexistent, at least in the urban area, and the gritty-tasting scrambled eggs he was occasionally served were made from powdered eggs. Even potatoes were rationed.

After their arrival in Great Britain, the group divided into small teams. During the next three weeks, Billy and Chuck toured England, Scotland, and Wales, while the other teams went to the European Continent. Billy and Chuck joined them at the beginning of April, and together they all toured Holland, Denmark, Belgium, and France. The landscape they traveled through was pockmarked and scarred from all the fighting. And as in London, many buildings had been reduced to rubble, along with bridges and roads. Valiant rebuilding efforts were in progress, but Billy could see that it would be some time before the scars of World War II were removed from the landscape. As Billy had noticed in Great Britain, the end of the war had fueled hope for the future in some people and despondency in others. He was aware of how blessed the United States was not to have experienced the extensive damage Europe had.

As he thought about home, more than anything, Billy wished that Ruth were at his side. She was home in North Carolina with baby Gigi, and he was eager to get back there to see them both.

The plane ride back to the United States was uneventful. After a visit to Montreat, Billy hit the road again. It was now summer, and YFC was hosting rallies across the country. Yet as Billy traveled the country preaching, his mind was never far from the trip to Europe, particularly Great Britain. There was so much more work to be done there—so many people were alone and desperate to hear good news. He began to pray that God would send him back. He discussed the idea with Torrey, but Torrey was not encouraging. "That would cost a lot of money, Billy," he said. "I don't think we can afford it. If you want to go there, you will have to raise the money yourself."

Billy set to work. By the end of summer he had raised the money and had a team ready to go with him. Once again Gavin Hamilton went on ahead to set up meetings, and Billy asked a husband-and-wife team, Cliff and Billie Barrows, to take charge of the music. He even convinced Ruth to leave Gigi with her family and join him once the rallies were under way in England.

In late September, Billy Graham and Cliff and Billie Barrows boarded a ship in New York, bound for Southampton, England. This time Billy was confident he knew how to reach English audiences, and he was right. The YFC rallies soon became a sensation as people flocked to hear Billy Graham preach. The rallies were held in halls, churches, even movie theaters after the last movie of the night had been shown. Billie Barrows would play the piano while Cliff led the crowds in stirring hymn singing before Billy got up and preached the gospel as clearly and simply as he could. After each sermon Billy gave an altar call, and people would march to the front for prayer to receive Jesus Christ.

Ruth flew to England to join Billy on December 9, 1946, just as an unusually chilly snap of weather engulfed the country. Snow lay on the ground, and it was bitter cold. Soon after Ruth's arrival, it was so cold that fog gathered inside one old stone church, making it impossible for Billy to see through the crowd to the back of the room.

It wasn't only churches and halls that were cold. Many homes had no heating, since gas was in short supply. Sleeping under these conditions became a challenge for Billy and Ruth. Billy took to wearing long woolen underwear beneath his flannel pajamas, over which he pulled a bulky sweater and then his overcoat before getting into bed. Beside him Ruth was bundled up with her sweater and two pairs of pants under her pajamas, not to mention slippers and a rabbit fur hat she also wore to bed. The two of them still shivered for a good part of the night.

After over forty rallies, the Grahams and the Barrowses took a break and flew to France, where they toured Paris. They then traveled south to Nice, where it was warm and sunny, to spend Christmas on the shores of the Mediterranean. When they arrived, however, they learned that the hotel where they'd booked rooms had no reservation record. They were told that the only hotel in the area with vacancies so close to Christmas was the luxurious Balmoral Hotel, farther along the coast in Monte Carlo. Billy's heart sank. They didn't have that kind of money, and even if they did, would it be right to spend it on a pricey hotel?

Then Billy remembered something he'd been carrying around in his suitcase. Before leaving the

United States, a hosiery manufacturer in North Carolina had given him many pairs of women's nylon stockings. Nylon stockings were in short supply in Europe, and Billy soon formed a plan. The two couples took a train to Monte Carlo, where Billy asked to speak with the hotel manager. The result was just as he had hoped it would be. Billy handed over four pairs of stockings a day in exchange for two rooms and three meals a day for the four of them. The arrangement worked perfectly, and the YFC team enjoyed the luxuries of eggs, fruit, butter, real coffee, and meat.

Early in the New Year, the group headed back to drab, cold England. In February, just as the money was beginning to run out, Ruth returned home to be with Gigi. Because Billy still had two months of preaching planned, he wrote to the only person he knew with the $7,000 needed to finish the tour. R. C. Le Tourneau had made his money inventing and selling large-scale earth-moving equipment. Billy didn't know the man well, but he hoped Mr. Le Tourneau would recognize the Youth for Christ name and help out. Two weeks later a cashier's check for $7,000 arrived in the mail, and the evangelistic rallies around Great Britain continued.

At times it was a lonely existence for Billy, always being with strangers, staying in their homes, catching glimpses of their everyday lives, and wondering what Ruth and Gigi were doing back in Montreat. The letters he received from Ruth were a lifeline, especially the one in which Ruth wrote, "I feel closer to you than ever before. . . . Wherever you are, I go with you in mind and heart—praying for you continually. . . . Take good care of your precious self. There is so much yet to be done for God and so much love yet unexplored and unexperienced for us."

As Billy prepared to return home to the United States, he took great comfort in Ruth's words. He was grateful that his wife understood his calling. What he didn't know, and was about to discover, was that Ruth had a clearer understanding of his mission than he did.

Chapter 7

"Old-Time Religion Sweeps Los Angeles"

It was three o'clock on a September afternoon in 1947. Billy sat talking to a very sick old man, William Bell Riley, who lay on a couch in his living room. Billy had first met Dr. Riley in Temple Terrace, Florida, while a student at the Florida Bible Institute. Dr. Riley and his wife liked to spend part of the winter there, and Billy had sometimes caddied for him when he played golf. William Bell Riley was known as "the grand old man of fundamentalism," and now, at the age of eighty-six, he was a living legend. In 1902, when he was forty-one, Dr. Riley had founded a Bible school for young people in his congregation. The school developed into an institution known as Northwestern Schools and, later, Northwestern College located in Minneapolis, Minnesota. Dr. Riley had been the college's president since its founding.

Dr. Riley wasted no time in getting to the reason he had invited Billy to visit him. "They tell me I don't have much time left, son," he said, "and the thing that weighs heavily on my mind is who is going to take over Northwestern when I'm gone."

Billy nodded sympathetically. Dr. Riley had led the college with a strong hand for forty-five years. It was difficult to imagine someone else taking it over.

Raising his head off the pillow, Dr. Riley pointed his bony finger directly at Billy and said with a firm voice, "Billy, I want you to take over as president when I die."

Billy sat speechless. All sorts of ideas ran through his head. He was a twenty-eight-year-old evangelist with a bachelor's degree, not everyone's ideal candidate for a college president. Billy finally responded. "I don't have the experience," he said. "I know nothing about running a college, I only have a bachelor's degree. You must know that already."

The old preacher smiled, and his eyes gleamed with enthusiasm. "Yes, I know, but you are just what the college needs. I've heard you preach. You have a passion to win people for Christ. Our students need to learn from that. And you have a nationwide network of friends through Youth for Christ. Think of the prayer support and the numbers of young people you can influence to grow in their Christian faith." He paused for a moment to catch his breath and then waved his arm. "Don't worry about all that administration business. I have a strong staff, and there are fifty people on the board of directors. They're the ones who really get things done. You would just be a figurehead—a steadying force—handing the baton of evangelism on to another generation. Just think of it. We have 750 students—that's 750 future evangelists to influence and train!"

Hearing it put that way, Billy began to think that he could be a good fit as the new president. The thought lasted only for a moment, after which he snapped back to reality. His gut told him he had no place accepting such an offer, but he felt trapped. He'd been taught to respect his elders, especially godly people like Dr. Riley.

"Dr. Riley," Billy said gently, "I can't accept this responsibility. God hasn't shown it to me. But if it'll ease your mind, I'll take it on an interim basis in an emergency during the next ten months until the board finds a suitable permanent president."

"I knew you would, son. I knew you would," Dr. Riley said with a smile.

Billy walked out of the Riley house feeling that he had been handed a ticking time bomb rather than a mantle. He knew he was called to preach the gospel far and wide, but he questioned whether God intended him to do this by using his energy to educate and inspire young people to be evangelists. This question puzzled Billy, and he prayed that the board of Northwestern Schools would find a new president as soon as possible.

Back in Montreat, Ruth, who had just learned she was pregnant again, did not mince words when Billy told her what had happened. "You have no business being a college president," she snapped.

"Interim president," Billy corrected, feeling the sting of his wife's words, "and only if Dr. Riley dies in the next ten months."

"Well, interim then," Ruth said. "But it's not your calling, and it's not my calling to be a college president's wife. What were you thinking, Billy?"

Billy didn't quite know how to answer her question.

Three months later, on December 5, 1947, a phone call informed Billy that Dr. Riley had died. No other names had been put forward to fill his position, and so Billy was now William Franklin Graham, President of Northwestern Schools. Now twenty-nine, he was the youngest, and quite possibly the least educated, college president in the United States.

Billy headed up to Minnesota to see what could be done. He was in for a shock. The college had run along quite nicely for forty-four years using Jackson Hall, which belonged to the First Baptist Church, as its campus. But the year before, Dr. Riley had decided to embark upon a building program. As Billy toured the building site overlooking a small lake in Loring Park, he noted holes in the ground and pilings, but nothing else. "About the time of Dr. Riley's death, we ran out of funds to complete the project," George Wilson, the business manager who was showing Billy around, explained. Billy's heart sank. It would take thousands of dollars to finish the job.

Billy knew he needed help. He called his boyhood friend TW Wilson and asked if he would consider becoming his vice president. TW said he would, and now, Billy joked, not one but two farm boys from North Carolina were running the show. TW and his wife, Mary Helen, moved to Minnesota to live at the college. Ruth refused to move, and Billy could understand why. She was heavily pregnant, and in May 1948 gave birth to a second daughter, whom they named Anne. In anticipation of a growing family, earlier in the year Billy and Ruth had bought their own home, a two-story, white clapboard structure right across the street from Ruth's parents in Montreat. It cost $4,500, which they borrowed from the bank. With another child to care for, Billy was more grateful than ever that Ruth had extended family to help out. Although he had cut back a little on his traveling with Youth for Christ, Billy was spending most of the extra time in Minnesota.

Somehow Billy and Ruth made it all work. Using his contacts, Billy was able to raise the funds for the new building. Gigi and Anne thrived under the watchful eye of their grandparents, aunts, and uncles, and Billy's work as an evangelist continued to grow.

On September 25, 1949, Billy Graham, Cliff Barrows, and George Beverly Shea, along with Grady and Wilma Wilson, found themselves in Los Angeles. They had been invited by a local group, "Christ for Greater Los Angeles," to conduct a three-week-long evangelistic campaign in a huge tent that had been set up at the corner of Washington Boulevard and Hill Street in downtown Los Angeles.

Billy was nervous as the campaign got under way. Despite the fact that the tent could seat six thousand people, the crowds that showed up during the first two weeks of meetings were small. As a result there was little media coverage of the event. Most frustrating to Billy was that those who did show up night after night were mostly Christians, but Billy wanted to reach people who did not go to church. That all changed when a gambling, hard-drinking radio talk show host by the name of Stuart Hamblen invited Billy onto his talk show. Even though it was the most popular radio show on the West Coast, Billy hesitated. How would it look, he wondered, if he went on a show that was sponsored by a tobacco company? When he remembered how Jesus spent time with the sinners of his day, he agreed.

During the show Stuart asked Billy all sorts of questions about his life. He then surprised him with a statement to his audience. "Go down to Billy Graham's tent and hear the teaching. I'll be there too!" This was the last thing Billy had expected to hear, but he encouraged Stuart to come that night.

Stuart did show up for the meeting, along with several hundred radio show listeners. The next night the tent was more crowded than the night before, and Billy thought it would be a good idea to extend the meetings. Not everyone agreed. It took a large number of people—choir members, ushers, counselors, and cleaners—to keep the campaign going, and many of these people were tired. Billy prayed that before the last meeting on Sunday morning God would give them a clear sign as to whether the campaign should continue.

At four thirty on Sunday morning the ringing of the telephone in his room at the Langham Hotel awoke Billy. Bleary-eyed, he picked up the receiver.

He recognized Stuart Hamblen's voice on the other end of the line. Through deep sobs Stuart begged Billy to meet with him right away. Soon Stuart and his wife, Suzy, who was a Christian, were seated in Billy's room talking, while Ruth and Grady and Wilma Wilson prayed in the room next door. As they prayed and Billy talked, Stuart wept and turned his life over to Jesus Christ. It was an astonishing moment, and when everyone left an hour later, Billy was certain the campaign in Los Angeles was supposed to continue.

Later that Sunday morning, in the campaign tent in front of thousands of people, Stuart Hamblen declared his new faith. He talked about it constantly on his radio show. Soon thousands of people on the West Coast began to wonder what exactly went on at a Billy Graham campaign. Many of them came to find out for themselves.

One morning after the decision had been made to continue the campaign, Billy arrived at the tent to find the place crawling with reporters. This was a big surprise to him, as the press had pretty much ignored the campaign. "What's happening?" he asked one of the reporters.

"You've been kissed by William Randolph Hearst," the reporter replied.

Billy had never met Hearst and wondered how the newspaper publisher had learned about him and the campaign. Nonetheless, he soon learned that being kissed by William Randolph Hearst meant lots of news coverage. Reporters began showing up for what they soon dubbed the "Canvas Cathedral" and wrote stories about the meetings. Since Hearst owned numerous newspapers across the country, these stories were carried nationwide. Soon competing newspapers began reporting on the meetings.

By early November the campaign was in its sixth week. National news headlines proclaimed, "OLD-TIME RELIGION SWEEPS LOS ANGELES." And it was true. Hundreds of people were becoming Christians every night. Most were ordinary, everyday people. Others were famous enough to catch the attention of the ever-present reporters. The conversion of one man in particular—Jim Vaus—captured the nation's imagination. Following the invitation to come forward and receive Christ at the end of one meeting, Jim, tears streaming down his cheeks, came forward with his wife. A genius with electronics, Jim was reputed to be the private wiretap man for mobster Mickey Cohen. Reporters recognized him as he walked to the front, and a newspaper headline the next morning declared, "EVANGELIST CONVERTS VAUS, SOUND ENGINEER IN VICE PROBE."

Several days after his conversion, Jim visited Billy and reported that Mickey Cohen had told him he was happy about his conversion. Jim also asked Billy if he would be willing to meet with Mickey. Billy said he would. The next night he and Jim slipped secretly out of the tent after the campaign meeting. They drove together to Mickey's house in Brentwood. Over a bottle of Coca-Cola Billy shared the gospel with Mickey and prayed for him.

The November 14, 1949, issue of *Time* magazine featured a story on Billy and the Los Angeles campaign. In response to the article, more people began showing up at the meetings each night—so many, in fact, that the tent had to be extended and three thousand more chairs brought in. Then it had to be extended yet again.

As the campaign entered its eighth and final week, another famous person was converted, adding to the media frenzy. Louis Zamperini was a former track star who had represented the United States at the 1936 Olympic Games in Berlin. At the Games he reputedly climbed a flagpole and stole Adolf Hitler's personal flag. During World War II, Louie served as a bombardier on a B-24 Liberator bomber that was shot down by the Japanese over the Pacific Ocean. For forty-seven days he and two crewmates drifted in a life raft, avoiding the attacks of Japanese pilots who swept in low and shot at them. One crewmate died after thirty-seven days, while Louie and the other crewman were captured and put in a Japanese prisoner-of-war camp for two years. Despite being a famous athlete and decorated war hero, Louie Zamperini explained to Billy that his life had been empty. Then he heard the gospel preached and knew that he had to respond and give his life to Jesus Christ. As with Jim's conversion, news of Louie's conversion was reported in the newspapers across the country.

On Sunday afternoon, November 20, 1949, Billy stood to preach his last sermon at the Los Angeles campaign. Eleven thousand people were packed into the Canvas Cathedral for the meeting. Thousands more stood outside, trying to hear Billy speak. In the eight weeks the campaign had run, hundreds of thousands of people had heard the gospel preached, and thousands had responded to it by coming forward to accept Jesus Christ. Eighty-two percent of these people had never been to church. Thousands more Christians had come to the front to renew their commitment to the Lord.

Following the Los Angeles campaign, Billy boarded the Santa Fe *Super Chief* train for the trip back to Minneapolis. He was glad for the chance to rest on the train. The demands of the campaign had pushed him to the edge of exhaustion, yet all that had happened exhilarated him. He had come to Los Angeles two months before as a small-time preacher. Now he was leaving as one of the most recognized Christian men in the country. It was not something Billy had sought; he'd just been open for God to use. At each stop on the journey north, reporters swarmed the train, eager for one more photo or story about the handsome young evangelist who had stormed Los Angeles. As he rode along, Billy wondered if this would be the peak of his fame or if something bigger was about to happen.

Chapter 8

A Growing Ministry

Six weeks later Billy Graham and his evangelistic team were in Boston. On December 30, 1949, the headline for an article in the *Boston Herald* declared, "EVANGELIST HERE TO VIE WITH NEW YEAR'S FUN." The article went on to say that Billy Graham was "a youthful evangelist who thinks he can out-rival the convivial lures of a New Year's Eve with a Mechanic's Building religious rally tomorrow night."

Two days later the *Boston Globe* declared, "Although hotels, nightclubs and bars in the city were crowded last night, the largest gathering in all of Greater Boston packed Mechanic's Building to hear Rev. Billy Graham, crusader for Christ . . ." The crowds continued to flow into the building, and then the Opera House, and finally Boston Garden, where on January 16, 1950, thirteen thousand people attended a campaign meeting. Newspaper reporters concluded that Billy Graham's Los Angeles campaign was not a fluke, after all. Billy was in the national spotlight for the long haul.

Still, even Billy was surprised when Henry Luce, founding editor and publisher of *Time* and *Life* magazines, announced plans to spend three days at Billy's next crusade in Columbia, South Carolina. Billy learned that Henry, one of the richest and most influential men in America, was the son of Presbyterian missionaries to China. Henry had attended the China Inland Mission school in Chefoo, which Hudson Taylor founded. Henry spent many hours chatting with Ruth about their similar experiences as missionaries' children and being raised in East Asia.

Like the previous two campaigns, the Columbia Crusade exceeded all expectations. Henry Luce was impressed with Billy's preaching. He assured Billy that he would endorse and promote his rallies in both *Time* and *Life*. Billy now began to sense that this life on the road as an evangelist was going to be permanent. As a result, it was time to think about organizing things better.

Thankfully, a team of crusade organizers was beginning to emerge. In Columbia, Willis Haymaker, a former banker, and Tedd Smith, a gifted pianist who also had wonderful administrative skills, agreed to add their expertise to the crusades. Right away, Billy deployed Tedd to travel ahead to the next crusade spot and prepare for the team's arrival.

Billy then headed back to Boston for a follow-up crusade and a preaching tour throughout New

England. He planned to end his time in New England on April 23, 1950, with a large gathering on Boston Common. He called the event a peace rally because he planned to address the fears many Americans were feeling. The end of World War II had not heralded the arrival of a peaceful and united world. Rather, the world seemed more divided than ever. The year before, Communists had seized control of China, and there was tension on the Korean peninsula that looked like it could explode into a war that would surely involve the United States. In addition, what was being called a Cold War had developed, with the United States and Western Europe on one side, and the Soviet Union and the Communist countries of Eastern Europe on the other.

Tensions were high, especially since both the United States and the Soviet Union had atomic bombs. The damage two American atomic bombs had inflicted on Japan at the end of World War II was fresh in people's minds. Many were terrified of what might happen if all-out atomic war broke out between the Soviet Union and the United States. Billy wanted to set people's minds at ease by offering them hope through Jesus Christ.

On the Sunday morning of the peace rally, Billy awoke to pouring rain that threatened to disrupt the outdoor rally on Boston Common. He gathered several members of his team together, and they prayed and asked God to clear away the rain by the time the rally started mid-afternoon. After they had prayed, Billy felt confident about the weather. Sure enough, when he stood to preach to the crowd of fifty thousand people who had gathered for the event, the sun shone brightly overhead.

From Boston, Billy and his team headed west to Portland, Oregon. Volunteers in Portland had erected a wooden tabernacle seating twelve thousand people, but the structure proved too small. Half a million people attended the six-week crusade, and a total of nine thousand people came forward at the end of the meetings to signify they wanted to become Christians.

As Billy and the team became more organized, they experienced many firsts during the Portland Crusade. It was the first time that sign-language interpreters were used, the first time that special separate meetings were held for men and women, and the first time that a crusade was filmed and edited. The documentary made during the Portland Crusade got Billy thinking: *What about making a movie based on a fictional character who becomes a Christian, and pitching it to young people?* The idea caught on, and since the next major crusade was scheduled for Fort Worth, Texas, Billy and his team decided to make a movie about a Texas rodeo rider who would become a Christian at a Billy Graham crusade. Soon production of the movie, to be called *Mr. Texas*, was under way. Two actors were hired to play the lead roles of Jim and Kay. The film also featured Billy, Cliff Barrows, George Beverly Shea, and Grady Wilson.

Other media beckoned as well. In 1950, television was a novelty. There were about five and a half million television sets in the country, along with 103 television stations spread across sixty cities. While the number of people watching television was growing rapidly, most Americans still relied on the radio for their news and entertainment. At the time, the largest radio broadcast, secular or religious, was *The Lutheran Hour*, hosted by Walter Maier. In mid-January, Dr. Maier died of a heart attack. On learning of his death, Billy began praying that God would raise up someone to take Dr. Maier's place. He never imagined that man might be him.

While Billy was in Portland, Fred Dienert and Walter Bennett visited to talk to him about starting a national radio show along the lines of *The Lutheran Hour*. The men estimated such a program would cost a lot of Billy's time and $7,000 a week to keep it on the air nationwide. Billy was not interested in their proposal and soon became annoyed when the two young men started showing up at his hotel, in the elevator, at the back of the stage, anywhere they could think of to attract his attention and talk about their proposal. In the end Billy asked Grady Wilson to sit down with the men and make them understand that he was not interested in a radio show. The men finally got the message. "We've come to say good-bye," they told Billy as he hurried out of his hotel room. "We're going back to Chicago tonight."

"All right," Billy said with a laugh. "If before midnight I should have $25,000 given to me to join your radio broadcast, I'll take that as a yes and contact you."

The two men also laughed. Twenty-five thousand dollars was an outrageous sum of money to come up with in a few hours. Everyone knew that getting it was out of the question.

That night more that seventeen thousand people showed up at the crusade meeting. Bob Pierce, a former evangelist with Youth for Christ who had just founded a Christian organization called World Vision, was about to speak about his observations on a recent trip to the Far East. But first, Billy stepped to the microphone and told the crowd about his encounter with Fred Dienert and Walter Bennett and how he had jokingly agreed to do a radio program if he received $25,000 by midnight.

After the meeting, people came to talk to Billy. Even though what he'd said about a radio show was not meant to be taken seriously, many of these people urged him to consider doing it. They pressed money, checks, and pledges into his hand. Billy was flabbergasted. He began to wonder how much money he'd actually stuffed into his pockets.

When Billy finally had a chance to count the money, it came to $24,000. Now Billy had a dilemma to solve. The amount was $1,000 short of what he said he needed to have by midnight. Should he honor his promise if he did not get the full $25,000, or should he take it as a sign that he was not to move ahead? Billy was still thinking about the issue when he returned to his hotel. As he walked through the lobby, the clerk at the front desk handed him two envelopes. Billy opened them. They were from people he hardly knew, Howard Butt and Bill Mead. The men had each written pretty much the same message. They both believed that Billy should go into radio, and they wanted to be the first to write a check to help him. Each man had enclosed a check for $500. There was now $1,000 to take the total to $25,000. Billy had his answer.

As he turned to get on the elevator, Billy discovered Fred Dienert and Walter Bennett standing in front of it. "I thought you had gotten on a plane tonight," he said.

Fred shook his head, then replied, "We got as far as the airport, but we couldn't take the flight. Something told us to come back and see you."

"Well, boys," Billy said, clapping his hands on their shoulders. "Sign us up for the radio for thirteen weeks. We have the $25,000, so we'll step out in faith."

Back in his hotel room Billy realized he had a problem as he tucked the money into a shoebox and slid it under his bed. He knew the money could not stay there, but what should he do with it? It was ministry money given for a specific purpose. If he deposited it into his own bank account, the money would be taxed. Yet he could not put it in the crusade account, because the organizing committee that invited him to come to Portland had set that up and the money in it was to be used to cover the cost of the crusade. So what should he do with the money for the new program, which would be called *Hour of Decision*? Billy knew it was time to start a separate organization to oversee the radio show, the movies, and any other future projects that came up.

The next day Billy called George Wilson, the business manager at Northwestern Schools, and asked him to look into the matter. Soon a formal nonprofit corporation was set up, with its headquarters in an office in Minneapolis, right across the street from Northwestern Schools. George suggested they call the new organization the Billy Graham Evangelistic Association, but Billy objected. He did not want his name front and center. The other members of his team agreed with George. Billy was the heart and soul of the movie they were making, and he would be the host of the new radio show. People all over the United States knew and trusted him. Billy finally agreed to the name, though he was not comfortable with it.

The first members of the board of directors of the Billy Graham Evangelistic Association (BGEA) were Cliff Barrows, Grady Wilson, George Wilson, and Billy Graham. Billy was grateful to have such a strong support team, all of whom he counted as friends and coworkers. The board was appointed in the nick of time. Once the *Hour of Decision* radio show went on the air, a lot had to be done. Mail and donations flowed in to the office. Every letter was answered, and every donation was acknowledged with a receipt and a thank you note. Soon George Wilson resigned from his position at Northwestern Schools and began working full-time as business manager for the BGEA.

The establishment of the Billy Graham Evangelistic Association did not solve all of the organization's money problems. In Atlanta in November 1950, the press challenged Billy's way of dividing up the money after a crusade. Some team members received a stipend, while Billy and Cliff Barrows, the two main speakers at the crusades, had their living expenses covered by the offerings. The rest of the money went to pay for expenses such as publicity, the tents, and electricity. If all of these expenses were paid in full, the last offering of the crusade was divided between Billy and Cliff, with Billy getting 60 percent of the total and Cliff 40 percent. In Atlanta, the last offering amounted to a lot of money—more than most people earned in a year. Billy and Cliff divided up the money as usual. Billy gave away one third of what he received to Christian causes and tucked the rest away for him and Ruth to buy a piece of land on the mountain behind their current home.

Although Billy had a clear conscience about the offering and how he spent the money, he knew that other people might see it differently. He did not intend to get rich preaching the gospel, and he did not want it to look that way. He turned to various friends for advice, and together they came up with a solution. Within the BGEA there would be no more offerings for preachers—including Billy. Instead, all the money from the offerings would go into a general fund from which Billy and Cliff, like the other members of the team, would be paid a salary. The salary would be a reasonable amount, about the same as a pastor in a large church would receive. Everyone agreed that this was a fair solution, and Billy was relieved. He did not want any confusion or misunderstanding about his motives for preaching.

By the end of 1950, Billy was able to look back with astonishment at what had been accomplished.

Over one and a half million people had come to hear
him preach, and around fifty thousand of those people had come forward for prayer. Additionally, the
BGEA had been founded, a movie made, a national
radio program launched, and most importantly, a
strong team had formed around Billy. It had been
a whirlwind of a year. Billy wondered what would
happen if things kept growing at the rate they had
during 1950. In the meantime he looked forward to
spending Christmas with Ruth and the children,
especially the newest addition to the Graham family,
little Ruth, or Bunny as she was soon nicknamed.
Ruth had been born on December 19, 1950, and
now Billy was the proud father of three girls.

Chapter 9

The Kind of Man the United States Needed

Early in 1951 Billy was in Fort Worth, Texas, for a large crusade. It was during this time that the movie *Mr. Texas* was released. The movie was well received, but as Billy watched it, he thought of ways it could be improved. He began thinking about the next movie to make.

Every month throughout the remainder of 1951, Billy and his team were in a different city in the United States holding crusades. Invitations to come to still more cities rolled in as the 1952 schedule began to fill up.

As he traveled the country, Billy read newspapers to keep himself abreast of what was going on with the war in Korea. From 1910 until the end of World War II in 1945, Korea had been ruled by Japan. With the end of the war and the defeat of Japan, Korea was divided in half at the thirty-eighth parallel. The north became the Communist-controlled Democratic People's Republic of Korea, supported by the Soviet Union, while the south became the Republic of Korea, supported by the United States and the United Nations. Much tension had developed between the two Koreas, and on June 25, 1950, the north invaded the south. The Soviet Union boycotted an urgent United Nations Security Council meeting called to discuss the situation in Korea. The United States then pushed for the Security Council to pass a resolution authorizing military intervention in Korea. Since the Soviets were not present to veto the resolution, it passed easily.

Within days, an international military force, of which nearly 90 percent were American soldiers, arrived on the Korean peninsula to help push back invaders from the north. The international army drove North Korean troops north to the Yalu River, which formed the border between North Korea and China. Then Communist Chinese forces joined the fight on the side of the North Koreans. By the end of 1951, the war was stalemated along the thirty-eighth parallel. Billy was saddened that so many people had been killed and wounded in the fighting, and there was no end in sight.

In early 1952 after a crusade in Washington, Billy, accompanied by Ruth, Cliff and Billie Barrows, and T. W. Wilson, traveled to Great Britain and Germany to make arrangements for crusades in both countries.

Back in the United States in August, Billy found himself seated in a room at the Brown Palace Hotel in Denver, Colorado, for a meeting. He looked into the gray-blue eyes of the man seated across from him. "Sir," Billy said, "do you still respect the religious teachings of your father and mother?"

"Yes," the man replied, lowering his eyes, "but I've gotten a long way from it."

Billy nodded. Some evangelists would have been more cautious while talking to the man who could be the next president of the United States, but Billy felt energized. He liked General Dwight D. Eisenhower as a person and was eager to offer him the opportunity to reexamine the reasons why he did not attend church anymore. Billy knew that the general had grown up in a strict churchgoing family, but now Dwight and his wife, Mamie, hardly ever went to church.

"I became disillusioned with the church early on, when some preachers seemed to care about money and status more than their faith," Dwight confided, "but I've been thinking about it, and as soon as the election is over I'm going to join a church."

"Wonderful," Billy said. "Why wait? Why not now?"

"I'm not going to do it in order to get elected. I don't want to use the church politically," the general said.

"What denomination do you have in mind?" Billy asked.

"Mamie's a Presbyterian, so I thought I would become one too. Can you suggest a church in Washington?"

Billy recommended several, including National Presbyterian, where an ex-military chaplain was the pastor.

"I'll do it," Dwight said, "and I'd like you to work on some of my speeches with me. I want more of a religious note in my campaign speeches."

"I'd be happy to help," Billy said, "but I don't want it splashed everywhere. I don't want to get a reputation for being for one party or the other."

"Fair enough," General Eisenhower said. "I would appreciate any help you can give me."

Billy was happy to do what he could to help. He especially liked that Eisenhower and his running mate, Richard Nixon, had taken a stand opposing discrimination against "race, religion, or national origin." Next to the war in Korea, which General Eisenhower promised to end speedily if elected president, the biggest struggle in the United States was for racial equality. In almost every way, black people were treated as second-class citizens. Those in government jobs were paid lower wages than their white counterparts, and blacks were not allowed to eat at the same restaurants or mix with whites in many public places. Given the prevalent racism they encountered, black people were beginning to band together and call for change, but it came at a terrible cost. In the previous year, groups of white men had bombed the homes of forty black families in the South, killing many people inside those homes. Billy was grateful that Eisenhower acknowledged the discrimination that black people endured and promised to do something about it.

For his part, Billy found it hard to understand such racial hatred. While he had been raised in the South, he had been taught to respect all people. His father had set an example, hiring a number of both blacks and Mexicans to work on the dairy farm. He had paid them well for their labor. In fact, his foreman on the farm, Reese Brown, was the highest-paid foreman in the district, earning four times as much as other black foremen. Many surrounding farmers complained to Billy's father about the amount he paid Reese. Billy's father simply told them that a good worker deserved a good wage in return for his labor. Besides, just like the white farmers, Reese had a family to support. Billy's father's example of how to treat people had imprinted deeply into Billy. Indeed, Reese's wife had been like a second mother to him, and Billy used to enjoy spending time with the Brown family.

From Denver Billy returned home to Montreat, eager to tell Ruth about his encounter with Dwight D. Eisenhower. He was also eager to spend time with the newest member of the Graham family, William Franklin Graham III, their first son, who had been born on July 14, 1952. As he made his way home to North Carolina, Billy was grateful that earlier in the year he had resigned as the president of Northwestern Schools. He had more than enough preaching assignments to keep him busy without the added burden of continually traveling to Minneapolis to oversee the college.

After a brief visit home, Billy hit the road again. He held more citywide crusades and was doing the weekly *Hour of Decision* radio broadcast. *Songs in the Night* was also proving to be a great success. Initially Billy had signed up for thirteen weeks, but now the show was a regular, ongoing part of his ministry. With the growth of television across the country, Billy was making appearances on several television shows. He was also involved in a book-writing project, with which Ruth was helping. The book was intended to present the gospel in a simple yet detailed way for readers who had little or no religious background.

On November 4, 1952, while Billy was holding a crusade in Albuquerque, New Mexico, Americans went to the polls to elect a new president. When the votes were tallied, Dwight Eisenhower had been elected president by a landslide, receiving thirty-four million votes and carrying thirty-nine states. His opponent, Adlai Stevenson, received twenty-seven million votes and carried nine states. Billy was pleased with the result. He felt that Dwight Eisenhower was the kind of man the United States needed as its president.

By now, Billy was looking forward to two weeks off at Christmas. That is, until he started receiving a stream of letters from missionaries, chaplains, and enlisted men, asking him to visit Korea. When Billy got a letter from Bob Pierce, founder of World Vision, offering to accompany him to Korea, he was conflicted. He had planned a quiet, country Christmas with Ruth and their four children. As he thought about all the men and women serving their country in Korea over Christmas, his heart went out to them. He asked Ruth what she thought he should do.

"Go," she told him. "Spend Christmas with our troops. We'll manage here."

Billy felt enormously grateful to have such a supportive wife.

On December 7, 1952, Billy, Bob Pierce, and Grady Wilson boarded a Boeing 377 Stratocruiser and flew out of Hawaii for Japan, the first stop on their tour to Korea. After a fuel stop at Wake Island, they took to the air again for the long haul to Tokyo. Although the plane was several hours late arriving in Tokyo, a large group of Japanese and foreign Christians met it at the airport. They held banners that read, "Welcome Billy Graham to Japan."

General Mark Clark, Commander of UN and US Army forces in the Far East, also welcomed the men. General Clark conferred on Billy the field rank of major general. This meant that Billy had access to all military sites in Japan and Korea. In addition, General Clark arranged for all of the men's needs to be taken care of, including food, transportation, even the heavy-duty boots and coats they would need in Korea.

Before heading for Korea, Billy and the others visited wounded American soldiers in Tokyo General Hospital. It was difficult for Billy to see the men suffering from terrible injuries as a result of the war. Some were paralyzed, others had arms and legs blown off, and some had been blinded. While in Japan Billy spoke at a banquet for 750 missionaries serving in Japan, and he also met with American chaplains. On December 14, after broadcasting the *Hour of Decision* radio show from Tokyo, Billy,

Grady, and Bob flew to Korea, where they landed in Pusan in the south.

The situation in Korea was very different from that in Japan. Billy saw devastation from the war everywhere, not to mention armaments and soldiers all around. He found the Koreans to be warm and friendly, just as Ruth had told him they would be, despite the mayhem that had engulfed their country. The children had broad smiles and were grateful for anything they were given. Yet Billy soon learned that behind the warm and friendly smiles lay despair and fear. The Koreans were unsure about how the outcome of the war would affect their lives.

Billy traveled with a military escort throughout South Korea, meeting and preaching to local people and soldiers alike. He visited Korean churches and UN military bases, where he mingled with the men over meals, thanking them for their service and answering their questions. He also preached in chapel services and visited the wounded, encouraging them in their recovery.

On Christmas Eve Billy visited a MASH (Mobile Army Surgical Hospital) unit a mile behind the front line in the war. He went from bed to bed, meeting the wounded soldiers, encouraging them, and wishing them a merry Christmas. The body of one young American soldier was so badly mangled from his injuries that he was forced to lie facedown in a bedlike contraption made of canvas and steel. All the soldier could do was stare at the floor.

"I doubt he'll ever walk again," a doctor whispered to Billy, pointing to the wounded young man.

Billy walked over and talked to the young man. As he turned to leave, the man said, "Mr. Graham, could I see your face? We've all been praying for you and looking forward to your visit. But I won't be able to be at the service tonight."

Billy lay on the floor and slid under the bed so that he was looking up into the soldier's eyes. As he prayed for the soldier, he could see tears welling in the young man's eyes.

Having seen so many wounded young men, Billy hoped that President Eisenhower would remain true to his word and end the war soon.

The tour of Korea ended on Christmas Day. Before leaving, Billy had the opportunity to meet with Major John Eisenhower, son of the president-elect. At the meeting they had their photo taken together, and Billy tucked it away in his bag to show General Eisenhower when he got back to the United States.

Three weeks after his return from Korea, Billy was at the Commodore Hotel in New York City with General Dwight Eisenhower, who would be sworn in as the thirty-fourth President of the United States in five days, on January 20, 1953. The general stood by the window, peering down at Grand Central Station. "You know, Billy," he said, "I think one of the reasons I was elected was to help lead this country spiritually. We need a spiritual revival."

"Yes, sir," Billy said. "I believe that."

"And," Eisenhower continued, "I want to start off strong. I'm going to have a worship service for the incoming administration, and I want you to help me find one or two appropriate passages from the Bible to use in my inaugural speech."

Billy suggested two verses, 2 Chronicles 7:14 and Psalm 33:12, choices that Dwight Eisenhower seemed happy with. When Billy attended the swearing-in ceremony at the East Portico of the US Capitol in Washington later that week, he was surprised and delighted that Eisenhower had gone even further. It was normal to have prayers at a presidential inauguration. What was not normal was for the incoming president to offer one himself. Yet Billy listened intently as President Eisenhower began his speech.

My friends, before I begin the expression of those thoughts that I deem appropriate to this moment, would you permit me the privilege of uttering a little private prayer of my own. And I ask that you bow your heads: Almighty God, as we stand here at this moment, my future associates in the executive branch of government join me in beseeching that Thou will make full and complete our dedication to the service of the people in this throng and their fellow citizens everywhere. Give us, we pray, the power to discern clearly right from wrong, and allow all our words and actions to be governed thereby and by the laws of this land. Especially we pray that our concern shall be for all the people regardless of station, race, or calling. May cooperation be permitted and be the mutual aim of those who, under the concepts of our Constitution, hold to differing political faiths, so that all may work for the good of our beloved country and Thy glory. Amen.

For a moment the sun peeked through the overcast sky as Billy listened closely to Eisenhower's speech.

For our own country, it has been a time of recurring trial. We have grown in power and in responsibility. We have passed through the anxieties of depression and of war to a summit unmatched in man's history. Seeking to secure peace in the world, we have had to fight through the forests of the Argonne, to the shores of Iwo Jima, and to the cold mountains of Korea.

In the swift rush of great events, we find ourselves groping to know the full sense and meaning of these times in which we live. In our quest of understanding, we beseech God's guidance. We summon all our knowledge of the past and we scan all signs of the future. We bring all our wit and all our will to meet the question: How far have we come in man's long pilgrimage from darkness toward light? Are we nearing the light—a day of freedom and of peace for all mankind? Or are the shadows of another night closing in upon us?

Billy nodded slowly as he heard the words. He sensed that the president had a grasp of the realities that lay before the country. He felt that the United States was nearing the light, but the country had some issues to deal with before fully entering that light to enjoy a "day of freedom and of peace for all mankind." One of the issues that he felt would be a hard fight over the next few years was the struggle of black people to gain their full rights as citizens of the United States.

Twelve days after the inauguration, Billy was delighted to learn that, true to his word, Dwight Eisenhower was baptized on February 1, 1953, at the National Presbyterian Church in Washington, DC, where he became an active member. He was the first president to be baptized in office.

Chapter 10

Common Ground

Billy Graham looked out as people began to flow into the stadium. It was March 15, 1953, the first night of the Chattanooga, Tennessee Crusade. Moments before, Billy had been sitting in the back room alone. He had resisted the urge to bite his fingernails and instead flipped through the Bible, hoping some verse would give him the strength he knew he needed. It had been two months since he'd attended Eisenhower's presidential inauguration, and Billy had been busy in the intervening months.

Always in the back of Billy's mind was the debacle in Jackson, Mississippi, the year before. Billy had pledged to integrate his crusades. He wanted blacks and whites to sit side by side in the stands as they listened to him preach. But things had not gone well when he tried to insist that the crusade be integrated. The leaders of many of the local churches who had helped organize the crusade chided him. "You're getting involved in local politics. We don't want a big mess to clean up when you leave. We're perfectly happy with going to separate churches and worshipping our own ways. Why would you want to change that?"

In his heart Billy felt that segregation was wrong, but he had not wanted to cause a public scene and so had backed down, saying, "I came to preach only the Bible and not to enter into local issues." Billy had always regretted that decision, and now, a year later in Chattanooga, he was rethinking his position. President Eisenhower had signaled that it was time to begin the movement toward full racial integration in the United States, and Billy was eager to play his part. "Eleven o'clock on Sunday morning is the most segregated hour in America," he had written in his notebook, "and it's time to challenge that. There is no scriptural basis for segregation, and I will not tolerate it in my crusades anymore. Everyone who comes to a crusade comes as an equal. The ground at the foot of the cross is level. Whites and blacks should stand shoulder to shoulder at the cross."

Now, as he stood and looked at the arriving crowd, Billy prayed for strength as he tucked his notebook into his pocket and walked out into the crowd. Many people recognized him from his publicity posters, and at six feet two inches tall, he towered above most men. He strolled purposefully toward the back, where several white men were hanging ropes with signs dangling from them that read, "No Blacks and Coloreds beyond this point. Whites Only." Billy grabbed one end of a rope and tugged on it.

"Hey, what are you doing?" asked the white man who had just strung up the rope.

"Do you know who I am?" Billy asked.

The man nodded. "Yes, but even being Billy Graham doesn't give you the right to pull down these ropes. The organizing committee asked me to put them here. They're in charge, not you," he added.

"Maybe so," Billy said, "but I'm telling you to take these barriers down and leave them down, or you can go on and have the revival without me."

That night and for the rest of the crusade, the rope barriers remained down. Black and white people stood together, sang together, listened together, and prayed together. And when Billy gave the altar call at the end of each meeting, they surged down the aisle together, often linking hands or arms. "There are no colors, no races in God's Kingdom," Billy encouraged those who attended the crusade meetings. "God looks at your heart, not the color of your skin."

A month later, at the end of the Chattanooga Crusade, Billy was convinced that he had done the right thing. Although so many things in the South were segregated, from schools to public playgrounds and even Woolworth's lunch counters, Billy knew he'd set a different standard for Christian meetings. There was still much to be done, but this was a start.

Following the crusade in Chattanooga, Billy kept busy with other crusades and evangelistic rallies throughout the United States. He traveled to St.

Louis, Missouri; Dallas, Texas; Syracuse, New York; Detroit, Michigan; and Asheville, North Carolina. In addition, he had begun a television version of the *Hour of Decision*, which ran on ABC Television. And the book he had been writing with Ruth's help was published in August 1953. Billy hoped that the book, titled *Peace with God*, would indeed help many people find peace with God.

As the end of the year approached, Billy looked forward to spending Christmas with his family, especially since he had been away in Korea the previous Christmas. Billy also looked to the challenges of the new year. A lot of behind-the-scenes preparation was under way for his 1954 tour of England and Europe, especially the citywide crusade to be held in London.

On February 19, 1954, Billy and Ruth Graham, along with six other members of the BGEA team, boarded the SS *United States* bound for Southampton, England. At thirty-five years of age, Billy felt too young and inexperienced for what lay ahead. It was one thing to preach to his fellow countrymen in the United States. It was quite another to set out across the Atlantic to hold a three-month-long, citywide crusade in the largest city in the world, with a culture quite different from that of the United States. Yes, he had preached in England before, but mostly in churches and evangelistic rallies. It had been nothing like the scale planned for this crusade. Billy was also well aware that a number of newspapers and some church leaders in England had predicted his downfall. "Billy Graham will return to the United

States with his tail between his legs," one Anglican bishop announced.

Before setting out from New York, Billy had called his friend Henry Luce at *Time* magazine. Henry had one piece of advice for him: "If you can get even an inch of coverage in the *Daily Mirror* or one of the big London dailies, that will help." Billy thanked him for his advice and began to pray that God would arrange for them to get media coverage in England.

As it turned out, Billy did not have to wait until the ship docked in Southampton to start getting British newspaper coverage. Regrettably, almost all of it was negative. While Billy was crossing the Atlantic, a scandal—with his name on it—had reached the boiling point in London. The first Billy heard of the scandal was on Monday morning, February 22, when the captain showed him a news report radioed to the ship. The report said that a member of the British Parliament was planning to challenge Billy's admission into the country. Billy had no idea why, but after a ship-to-shore phone call to the Billy Graham Evangelistic Association office in Minneapolis, things became clear. The entire situation had developed over a mistaken capital *S* in a prayer calendar sent out to supporters in the United States.

The text for the calendar had been written by a staffer at the BGEA office in Minneapolis who was unfamiliar with the political situation in Great Britain. As a result one line of the text declared, "What Hitler's bombs could not do, socialism, with its accompanying evils, shortly accomplished." The staffer had intended to convey *secularism* when he used the word *socialism*, unaware that the British Labor Party was also know as the Socialist Party with a capital *S*. When the printer set the type for the calendar, he had decided to capitalize the *S* at the start of *socialism* so that the line read, "What Hitler's bombs could not do, Socialism, with its accompanying evils, shortly accomplished."

When the typeset copy was proofread by another BGEA staff member who understood politics in Britain and realized the wording implied the British Labor Party, he quickly changed the line to read, "What Hitler's bombs could not do, secularism, with its accompanying evils, shortly accomplished." However, the printer failed to correct the mistake, which wasn't noticed until two hundred calendars had been printed. The change was then made, and the remaining calendars were printed. One of the two hundred misprinted calendars somehow made its way to England, where the textual error caused a fury. The Billy Graham Evangelistic Association formally apologized for the mistake, and Billy personally wired an apology from the ship.

When the SS *United States* arrived in Southampton on February 24, pandemonium had broken out at the dock. A tugboat laden with twenty-five newspaper reporters and twelve photographers pulled alongside the ship. Cameras started rolling while reporters yelled questions up at Billy. "Who invited you here, anyway?" "What makes you think England is in worse spiritual shape than America? Go home and fix your own problems." "Why does your wife wear makeup?" "Are you going on to preach in

Russia?" "How much money do you plan to make here?"

The questions kept coming, and Billy and Ruth descended the gangway. The couple answered as politely as they could, but every reply seemed to draw more angry questions. Eventually Billy and Ruth made it through customs and immigration. Billy was grateful for the small tokens of encouragement he received from several local people. One dockworker yelled, "I'm praying for you," and a customs officer shook Billy's hand warmly and said, "Welcome to England, and good luck, sir. We need you."

Cliff Barrows and several other crusade workers who had come ahead to set up for the crusade welcomed Billy and Ruth, Grady Wilson, and the Reverend Paul Rees and his wife at dockside. Cliff was unsure about all the negative press coverage the upcoming crusade was receiving, as was Billy. Yes, it was press coverage, but not the kind they had been hoping for.

The group spent the night in Southampton, where they took time to pray about the situation. The following morning they caught the train to Waterloo Station in London. The crowd waiting for them at the station was huge—the largest crowd to greet anyone in over forty years. Hymns rang out as Billy and Ruth climbed off the train. People waved welcome banners while reporters and photographers documented their arrival. Afternoon editions of the newspapers carried headlines such as, "FILM STARS—SO WHY NOT BILLY?" and "AMERICAN INVASION HAS BEGUN."

Thankfully, the advance team had done their job well, and everything was in place for the start of the crusade on March 1. Until then Billy kept busy with a number of different activities. First up was a press conference, followed by dinner with members of the British aristocracy, a luncheon with one thousand ministers, and a reception with Parliament members at the House of Commons. Since Billy's previous visit to England in 1952, Great Britain had crowned a new monarch. Following the death of her father, King George VI, the king's oldest daughter, at twenty-five years of age, was crowned Queen Elizabeth II on June 2, 1953. As he talked to British people at the various events he attended, Billy found that they genuinely admired their new queen.

Of course all of Billy's activities meant nothing if people did not turn out to hear him preach. He was a little worried in that regard. Billy was still receiving a lot of negative press, and he wondered if the newspaper coverage would keep people from crusade meetings. If people didn't show up, Billy, his team, and the organizing committee would all look like fools. But a meeting with the Bishop of Barking earlier in the day had encouraged Billy. The bishop had been criticized mercilessly in the newspapers for his endorsement of the crusade. With a smile, he said, "Don't worry about me, Billy. If for a few days the newspapers have made you appear a fool for Christ's sake, I shall be only too happy to appear a fool with you."

The opening day of the crusade arrived. Not only was the day cold, but also, to Billy's dismay, sleet

began to fall as the day wore on. Even though the
meetings were to be held indoors, Billy fretted that
the weather might keep people away. One of his
team members called to say that only a few people
had trickled in and press photographers were busy
taking photos of the rows of empty seats. Billy began
to despair. After he hung up the telephone, he got
down on his knees and committed the outcome of
the meeting to God. If few people showed up and the
newspapers did indeed brand him a fool for Christ,
Billy was content with that outcome.

Billy and Ruth were driven to Harringay Arena
in North London, about a half-hour drive from their
hotel. The Harringay Arena was the largest indoor
stadium in London. Billy had to admit the building
wasn't much to look at, inside or out. It was used
mostly for dog racing, ice hockey, netball, and cir-
cuses, but it could comfortably seat ten thousand
people. When the car pulled up to the arena, Billy
saw no stream of cars arriving or people lined up
to get into the meeting. As he stepped from the car,
Willis Haymaker, one of his associates, bounded up.
"The arena is jammed," he told Billy enthusiastically.

Billy looked puzzled. "What do you mean
'jammed'?" he asked. "I don't see many people
around."

"We're at the back of the arena," Willis informed
him. "On the other side, at the front entrance, hundreds of people are standing outside because the
arena is so full."

As Billy entered Harringay Arena, he was stunned.
The place was packed to capacity. The crowd was

singing hymns loudly as Billy walked to the platform and took a seat. That night Billy preached his
heart out, and over two hundred people came to the
front when he gave the invitation to come forward to
receive Jesus Christ.

By Saturday night of the first week of the crusade,
ten thousand people were packed inside Harringay
Arena, and another thirty thousand people were
gathered outside. People poured into London from
all over England to hear Billy preach. They jammed
the roads and railway stations. So many people were
showing up for meetings that the team began holding two a day on the weekends. The tide had turned.
Previously skeptical ministers began urging their
congregations to listen to Billy Graham preach. Also,
the negative tone of the news media had changed.
Requests for interviews with Billy poured in from the
BBC (British Broadcasting Corporation) and from a
host of English and European television stations,
radio programs, and newspapers. As well, a number of reporters from newspapers in other European
countries arrived in London to cover the crusade.

During a prayer meeting for the crusade, Charlie
Riggs, a member of the BGEA responsible for over-
seeing the counseling, prayed that God would give
them a way to reach out beyond London with the
crusade. A radio network engineer heard his prayer
and set to work on finding a way to do this. The
engineer discovered that during the war, the General
Post Office had strung up telephone-type message
lines throughout England. The lines were called
landline relays. They had speakers attached to them

so that messages about the war could be broadcast to the people of England. These lines were still in place, and the crusade was quickly able to negotiate use of them to broadcast crusade meetings to churches, halls, and theaters throughout the country. Soon four hundred lines ran out from Harringay Arena, carrying the crusade meetings far and wide.

Best of all, as the crusade progressed, Billy began hearing reports of people's lives being changed through the power of the gospel. Most of these people were ordinary folk, but some were famous. One of them was Joan Winmill, a well-known actress on the stage in London. She came to the front to accept Christ, and Ruth ended up counseling her. Joan didn't know who Ruth was, and after they had prayed and talked, Ruth asked Joan if she would like to meet her husband. Joan nodded, and Ruth led her down a long corridor, where she knocked on a door. Much to Joan's amazement, Billy opened the door. "This is Joan. She just made a decision for the Lord," Ruth said. "That's wonderful," Billy replied, smiling at the shocked look on the woman's face.

Others who responded to the message were war heroes like Richard Carr-Gomm. Richard came from a wealthy family and now served as a captain in the Queen's Guard at Buckingham Palace. Although he was a Christian, he felt it was time to do something more meaningful in his Christian walk. He came forward to publicly acknowledge this at the London Crusade.

Some of the stories were funny. Two strangers stood side by side and decided at the same time to accept Christ. As the two walked toward the front, one turned to the other and said, "I had no intention of going down the aisle until I heard Billy preach."

"Me neither," the second man replied.

"Well, then," the first man said, reaching into his pocket. "Here's your wallet back. I'm a pickpocket. I stole it at the beginning of the program."

And there was the man who arrived late and found the gate to the meeting locked. A youth who was standing around aimlessly asked the man if he needed help. The man lamented that he had arrived too late. "Don't worry about that," the youth said, pulling from his pocket a tool with which he proceeded to pick the lock. The man went into the crusade meeting and became a Christian that night.

As the weeks rolled on, the crusade continued to pick up momentum. A number of BGEA supporters from the United States turned up to help out. Among them were the entertainers Roy Rogers and Dale Evans, along with their horse Trigger. Roy and Dale held a meeting at the outdoor stadium next door, to which forty thousand boys and girls came. Henrietta Mears, a friend of Billy's and a well-known Bible teacher from Los Angeles, also came to pray for Billy and help him develop new sermons.

On May 22, 1954, twelve weeks after it had begun, the London Crusade ended. By now Billy was exhausted and fifteen pounds lighter because of so much activity. Since no indoor facility in London was large enough to hold the expected crowd at the final two meetings, the meetings were held in outdoor stadiums. Sixty-five thousand people attended the meeting held at White City Stadium. Hours later, 120,000 people packed Wembley Stadium for the final meeting. At the meeting, the Archbishop of Canterbury pronounced the benediction. As George Beverly Shea led the audience in singing "To God Be the Glory," tears rolled down Billy's cheeks. *Yes,* Billy thought, *to God be the glory, great things He has done.* Billy had arrived in England three months before under a cloud of suspicion. Now the people of Great Britain embraced him and his team as if they were family. In all, over two million people had come to hear Billy preach, and hundreds of thousands more had heard him live via landline transmission to churches and halls across England. And over thirty-eight thousand people had come forward at the end of the meetings to dedicate their lives to Jesus Christ.

As Billy left the platform that night, he overheard the Archbishop of Canterbury tell Grady, "We may never again see a sight like that this side of heaven." In his enthusiasm Grady threw his arm around the archbishop and said, "That's right, Brother Archbishop!" Billy smiled. As Americans, they may not have always used the proper names for people, bowed at the right times, or used the correct fork at formal dinners. In fact, Henrietta Mears had run out of time to get ready for an expensive reception at the Dorchester Hotel when she first arrived in England and had worn her nightgown with fancy accessories to the event. In spite of all of that, the "brash"

Americans and the "understated" British had found common ground in their Christian faith.

With the London Crusade over, it was time to move on. Other cities and other countries awaited the good news that Billy Graham and his team had to proclaim.

Chapter 11

Europe and Beyond

Three days after the end of the London Crusade, Billy sat in his hotel room. He'd already started packing, since he and his team would be catching a train to Scotland that evening. The phone rang, and Billy picked it up. "This is Jock Colville, secretary to Prime Minister Winston Churchill," said the voice at the other end of the line. "Mr. Churchill would like to know if you would be available to join him tomorrow at noon for lunch."

It took Billy a second or two to register whom he was talking to. "I'm honored, but it won't be possible," Billy replied. "My team and I are on our way to Scotland tonight."

"Very well," Jock said. "I shall convey your regrets to the prime minister."

As he hung up the phone, Billy wondered whether he'd done the right thing. Under normal

circumstances, he would have jumped at the opportunity to meet England's ultimate war hero and
prime minister during World War II. But in truth
Billy was totally exhausted. He could not imagine
delaying his trip to Scotland, where he would have
time to rest, by even one day.

He was still thinking about the call when the
phone in his hotel room rang a second time. It was
Jock Colville again. "Mr. Graham, would you be able
to meet with the prime minister at noon today? He
has a lunch scheduled for twelve thirty with the
Duke of Windsor, who is flying over from France, but
he can see you before that." This time Billy agreed.

At 11:50 a.m. Billy knocked on the door of Number
10 Downing Street, the official home of British prime
ministers. Jock Colville ushered Billy in, informing
him that Churchill had only twenty minutes to talk.
He asked Billy to double check his watch to make
sure it was accurate. Billy was then shown into the
wood-paneled cabinet room. The office was dimly lit,
and a long, wooden table with chairs on both sides
ran down the middle of the room. Churchill sat in a
leather chair at the middle of the table in front of the
fireplace. He stood as Billy entered the room, and
the two men shook hands. Billy was surprised at
how short the prime minister was, but he instantly
recognized the baritone voice he had heard on the
radio and in newsreels during the war.

"Sit down, sit down," Churchill said, motioning
Billy toward the chair next to him. "Let me congratu-
late you on the huge crowds you have been drawing."
He continued speaking while Billy sat down and,

picking up the day's copy of the *Guardian* newspaper, gestured toward a headline.

"It's God's doing, not mine," Billy said.

"That may be, but I daresay that if I brought American actress Marilyn Monroe over here, and she and I together went to Wembley, we couldn't fill it," the prime minister said dryly.

Billy chuckled.

"So tell me, Reverend Graham, what is it that packed Harringay Arena night after night?"

"I think it is the gospel of Christ," Billy replied, going on to tell the prime minister how in these uncertain times people were hungry to hear a word straight from the Bible.

"Yes, things have changed. Look at these newspapers. They're filled with nothing but murder and war and what the Communists are up to. You know, the world may one day very well be taken over by Communists," Churchill said.

Billy nodded, not wanting to be drawn into a discussion of global politics.

"I tell you, I have no hope. I see no hope for the world," the prime minister continued.

Billy looked Churchill in the eyes.

"I am a man without hope," Churchill said. "Do you have real hope?"

"Are you without personal hope as well?" Billy asked. "Hope for your own soul?"

Churchill nodded. "I have thought about that a great deal lately."

That was all Billy needed. He pulled out his small New Testament. As he began to explain the gospel and how a person finds salvation, he noticed that Churchill's eyes lit up.

At twelve thirty on the dot Jock knocked on the door to the cabinet room and informed the prime minister that the Duke of Windsor had arrived for their luncheon.

"Let him wait," Churchill snapped, motioning for Jock to leave the room.

Billy continued for the next fifteen minutes, praying with the prime minister before their meeting was over. Churchill shook Billy's hand firmly as they parted.

Billy was glad to have had the opportunity to talk with Winston Churchill and offer him words of hope. Now he looked forward to a few days' rest in Scotland, where he also planned to meet with ministers in Glasgow to investigate the possibility of holding a crusade there the following year.

Billy was able to spend some well-earned time relaxing with Ruth. When their minivacation was over, Ruth headed back to the United States. Meanwhile, Billy and three of his team members set sail for Sweden from Tilbury, England, to begin their European tour.

In Europe the BGEA had teamed up with the Greater Europe Mission, started by two of Billy's Wheaton College friends, Bob Evans and Jerry Beaven. In light of the huge crowds at Harringay Arena, some adjustments had to be made to the European tour. The venues were too small, and alternate, larger arenas were booked for the meetings. Instead of spending just one day per city as previously planned, the team decided to spend two days in each place.

The following two weeks were a whirlwind of activity. Billy preached in Helsinki, Finland; Stockholm, Sweden; Amsterdam, the Netherlands; and the German cities of Frankfurt, Dusseldorf, and Berlin. Everywhere Billy and his team went, huge crowds turned out. Over three hundred thousand people came to hear him preach while he was in Europe. Press reports in various countries carried articles that either welcomed Billy or ridiculed him for his American ways. In Germany one newspaper called Billy "God's machine gun," and another, "God's flamethrower." Meanwhile, the newspapers in Communist East Germany called Billy a tool of American capitalism and a spy for the Office of Strategic Services. Billy didn't mind. He was there to preach the gospel, and that was what he did.

The final meeting in Germany was held in Olympic Stadium in Berlin, where eighty thousand Germans came to hear Billy preach. Knowing that he was standing in the same stadium in which Adolf Hitler had inspired people to hatred and great evil, Billy stepped up to the podium and said, "Others have stood here and spoken to you." Then, holding up his Bible, he declared, "Now God speaks to you!" At the end of the meeting, sixteen thousand people filled out decision cards.

When Billy arrived back in the United States in the middle of summer, Ruth had a surprise for him. While Billy had been away on an earlier crusade, a property had come up for sale on a mountain ridge above Montreat, and Ruth had arranged to purchase it. The Grahams planned to one day build a new home for themselves there. Now that Billy was back from Great Britain and Europe, Ruth was eager to show him what she had done on the property in his absence. She drove Billy on the dirt road up the mountainside behind Montreat and pulled the Jeep to a halt in front of one of the old log cabins.

Billy was amazed when he walked inside the cabin. The interior was completely remodeled to be more spacious and a stone fireplace had been installed. Downstairs was a double bed, and upstairs in the loft, mattresses were laid out for the children to sleep on. It was all very rustic. The cooking would be done at the fireplace and on a grill outside, and a bathroom had been installed in an outbuilding a short distance from the cabin. Billy was impressed with what his wife had accomplished. Ruth explained to him that she wanted the remodeled cabin to be a retreat for the family until their new home was eventually built on the property.

Billy soon learned to appreciate the retreat. Since the London Crusade he had become an international celebrity, and people had flocked to Montreat to catch a glimpse of him and his family. It was not uncommon for the Grahams to find strangers peering in the windows of their house or to see tour buses rolling down the street. Some people even stripped nails from the front fence to keep as souvenirs. Being treated like a movie star was not something Billy wanted or enjoyed, and he was glad to be able to escape to the family retreat on the mountain.

A number of things had occurred in the United States while Billy had been away in Great Britain and Europe. The day before the start of the London Crusade, the United States had tested its first hydrogen bomb on remote Bikini Atoll in the western Pacific. This new type of bomb was multiple times more powerful than the atomic bombs dropped on Japan at the end of World War II. If used in a war, nuclear bombs had the power to destroy huge swaths of a country. While the United States now possessed these potent bombs, so did the Soviet Union. Billy noted an increased level of fear and angst about the possibility of war involving such destructive weapons.

There was other world news impacting Billy's work. On May 17, 1954 two and a half months into Billy's London Crusade, the United States Supreme Court had handed down a landmark decision known as *Brown v. Board of Education,* in which the court ruled that the segregation of public schools in America was unconstitutional.

Black people as well as many whites hailed the decision and looked forward to a new era of progress and opportunity. Sadly, the Supreme Court's decision was opposed in the South, where everyday segregation was a way of life. In Mississippi, which many considered the most segregated southern state, the decision did not sit well. An editorial in the *Jackson Daily News* called the court ruling "the worst thing that has happened to the South since carpetbaggers and scalawags took charge of our civil government in reconstruction days." It declared that desegregation would lead to "racial strife of the bitterest sort." The *Daily News*, another Mississippi newspaper, called for elected officials to fight the decision. It stated in its editorial, "Even though it was delivered by a unanimous vote of the nine members of the nation's highest tribunal, Mississippi cannot and will not try to abide by such a decision." Billy hoped that the decision would be accepted by southern states and that the nation could move forward in harmony by integrating its schools. For his part, he determined to continue making sure all of his crusades were integrated, with blacks and whites sitting together.

As he reflected on his time in Great Britain and Europe, Billy came to accept that the mission and influence of the Billy Graham Evangelistic Association now went far beyond the shores of North America. As a result the BGEA opened a permanent office in London and began planning a follow-up six-week crusade to Scotland as well as another two weeks of crusades in London in March 1955.

The meetings went ahead as planned, and Billy and his message once again drew huge crowds. The meetings were picked up and broadcast by the BBC. On Good Friday 1955, one of Billy's sermons from the Glasgow Crusade was seen live on television and heard on radio by a larger audience than had watched the coronation of Queen Elizabeth II. Billy soon learned that the queen herself had watched the broadcast. Afterward she invited him to Windsor Castle to preach.

While in England, Billy also met with C. S. Lewis, author of the Chronicles of Narnia series,

The Screwtape Letters, and other Christian books. The two met in the dining hall at Magdalene College, Cambridge, where they talked for more than an hour. When their time was over, C. S. Lewis looked at Billy and said, "You must know that you have many critics, but I have never met one of your critics who knows you personally."

Billy was grateful for the kind words from such a scholarly and well-respected Christian. He knew that many people, even some Christians, were critical of his direct approach to preaching the gospel. As he planned his next set of crusades, he was sure he would step on even more toes. This was because he was going somewhere new—not to a country with a strong Christian tradition but to a land with over four hundred million people of many different religions and cultures: India.

Back in the United States, in August 1955 Billy spent a day with President Eisenhower and his wife, Mamie, at their farm beside the Gettysburg battlefield in Pennsylvania. Dwight and Mamie liked to retreat from Washington, DC, to the farm on weekends. Billy ate lunch with the president in the large white farmhouse and was able to talk with him more about the Christian faith. Afterward they went upstairs, where Billy prayed for Mamie, who was not feeling well. Dwight then asked Billy if he would like to take a tour of the Gettysburg battlefield.

"Yes," Billy replied. "Both of my grandfathers fought there."

"Do you know which group they were with—North or South Carolina?" the president asked.

When Billy explained that he wasn't sure, President Eisenhower had him call his parents to find out.

At the battlefield the president drove Billy around in a golf cart, with members of the secret service following behind in another vehicle. As they drove, President Eisenhower explained what had occurred at the battle. Billy was impressed with his knowledge of it and other Civil War battles. Billy and the president also drove to the part of the battlefield where Billy's grandfather, Ben Coffey, had probably fought as part of Pickett's Charge.

Back at the farm Billy and the president sat in front of the fireplace and talked some more. President Eisenhower particularly wanted to know about heaven. Billy pulled out his New Testament and explained many Scripture passages that addressed it. After Billy had spent a wonderful day on the farm with the Eisenhowers, the president arranged for him to be flown in his private plane to Charlotte, North Carolina, where he was to preach that evening.

In mid-January 1956, Billy and a small team set out for India to hold crusades in Bombay, Madras, Kottayam, Palamcottah, New Delhi, and Calcutta. These cities had been chosen because they had pockets of local Christians who would support the crusade and welcome new converts into their churches afterward. Traveling with Billy was George Burnham, a former newspaper reporter from Chattanooga. George, a recovering alcoholic who had become a Christian, had six hundred newspapers signed up to carry the stories he planned to write about the India trip.

As the airplane flew toward India, Billy wondered what he could say to the people in that land. He had read that many Indians assumed Christianity was a "white man's religion" and did not take the time to understand it. Suddenly, somewhere over Egypt, the answer came to him. Jesus had been born in the Middle East, where Asia, Africa, and Europe intersect. He was not a white person, and the first missionaries—the apostles—were eastern people. In fact, according to tradition, Jesus's disciple Thomas had come to southern India in AD 52 and established Christian churches. Thus Christianity had old and deep roots in India. God was not a white man's God, and Christianity was not a Western religion. God loved everyone from all races and all cultures.

The first stop, in Bombay, was eye-opening for Billy. Riots were taking place in the streets of the city when the team arrived, and local Christian leaders warned Billy that it was too dangerous to hold public meetings. Billy spent the time walking the streets of Bombay, praying and meeting with local pastors. Even though he had been warned before leaving the United States, he was shocked by the extreme poverty. At first he felt he had to give a few rupees to anyone who begged for them on the streets. This notion soon changed when Billy was engulfed by a huge crowd of people fighting and screaming at each other to get closer to him and hopefully to get some rupees.

The situation was much different six hundred miles away in Madras, on the southeastern coast of the Indian subcontinent. In Madras, crowds of forty thousand people gathered from hundreds of miles around to hear Billy preach. The crusade messages and hymns were translated into Telugu and Tamil, the languages spoken in the region. Then it was on to Kottayam and Palamcottah.

While he was staying at Palamcottah, Billy made a side trip to Dohnavur, where the fellowship started by Irish missionary Amy Carmichael was located. Billy and Ruth had enjoyed Amy's devotional writings over the years and had prayed for her work in southern India. Billy was eager to see the fellowship orphanage where Amy had taken in Indian girls.

Amy had died five years before, but Dohnavur Fellowship was still going strong. As Billy was shown around the place, he was deeply moved. When he was asked to pray in the room where Amy Carmichael had died, Billy's eyes filled with tears, and he was unable to finish his prayer.

From Palamcottah in the south Billy headed north to New Delhi, India's capital. While in New Delhi, a meeting was arranged between Billy and Indian Prime Minister Jawaharlal Nehru. Nehru was an intelligent man who had been educated at Trinity College in Cambridge, England. He had served as prime minister since the country won independence from Great Britain in June 1947.

At first the meeting was awkward for Billy. The prime minister said nothing and waited for Billy to speak. After some time Billy thanked Nehru for agreeing to the meeting and proceeded to give a summary of his time so far in India. Still the prime minister said nothing. Billy tried a different approach.

He told Nehru what Christ meant to him and how Jesus had changed his life. At this, the prime minster's attitude changed. His face lit up, and he began peppering Billy with questions about his faith. Billy could tell from the questions that Nehru had a good grasp of the beliefs of Christianity. When the meeting was over, Nehru commended Billy for the good work he was doing in India.

In New Delhi Billy also met Dr. Akbar Abdul-Haqq and was deeply impressed by the depth of his Christian faith. Akbar Abdul-Haqq had been born in India and was a graduate of Northwestern University near Chicago. He spoke perfect English as well as the local Indian languages, and Billy asked him to be his interpreter during the New Delhi crusades. Following the New Delhi Crusade, Billy invited Akbar Abdul-Haqq to join his crusade team as an associate evangelist and move to the United States.

From India, Billy traveled on to Thailand, the Philippines, Hong Kong, and Japan to hold evangelistic meetings before heading back to the United States. Along the way, George Burnham took notes, which he told Billy he intended to turn into a book when they got home. In the eight weeks he had been away, Billy had learned a great deal about the Christian church in Asia, and he knew for sure that he wanted to return and preach some more.

Once back home in the United States, Billy turned his attention to launching another project he had been thinking about. Billy was concerned that there was no magazine for evangelical Christian leaders. He envisaged a magazine for pastors, seminary students, and interested Christian leaders that combined thorough news coverage with thoughtful and insightful articles on evangelical theology and issues facing the church. His father-in-law, Dr. Nelson Bell, while continuing his medical practice in Asheville, North Carolina, had helped start a magazine called the *Presbyterian Journal*. He knew the steps that needed to be taken to get a new publication off the ground. He agreed to help Billy with the project, serving as executive editor of the magazine, which would be called *Christianity Today*. Carl F. Henry, who had been a graduate student at Wheaton College when Billy attended the school and who had journalistic experience, agreed to become the magazine's managing editor.

On July 30, 1956, Billy learned that President Eisenhower had signed a new law into effect. According to the new law, the phrase "under God" was to be inserted into the Pledge of Allegiance. Also, the phrase "In God We Trust," which had been placed on US coins since the Civil War, was to become the nation's official motto and would henceforth be printed on all American paper currency. Billy was pleased. He felt it was good for the country to be reminded of its Christian roots and that a greater trust in God would help strengthen the United States. He also realized, however, that a new motto alone would not solve the problems the nation grappled with. Solving these problems would take a change of heart on the part of many people.

On October 15, 1956, Billy was preaching at a crusade in Louisville, Kentucky, when he received the first issue of *Christianity Today*. He was delighted by both the look of the magazine and its content. He had written an article titled "Biblical Authority in Evangelism" for the first edition. As he thumbed through the magazine, Billy hoped that it would be widely accepted within the evangelical community and would encourage Christians, particularly pastors, to boldly declare their faith.

Chapter 12

New York, New York

We are not here to put on a show or an entertainment," Billy said, looking out over the
crowd of twenty thousand New Yorkers. "We believe
that there are many people here tonight who have
hungry hearts. All your life you've been searching for
peace, joy, happiness, and forgiveness. I want to tell
you, before you leave Madison Square Garden this
night of May 15, 1957, you can find everything you
have been searching for in Christ."

It was the first night of the long-anticipated New
York City Crusade, and the press coverage was
intense from the start. Three hundred reporters,
photographers, and camera operators descended on
Madison Square Garden to cover every word Billy
uttered. They followed him around town, snapping
photographs of everything—from the hotdog he

bought from a Times Square vendor to Billy talking one-on-one with the men and women on The Bowery, Manhattan's skid row.

Even before it began, the New York City Crusade had cost Billy dearly. During the planning Billy had learned that over half of the eight million residents did not have any religious affiliation; 27 percent were Catholic, 10 percent Jewish, and only 7.5 percent Protestant. As he thought about the planning and work required to conduct such a large campaign, Billy realized that he would need the backing of all the Christian churches in the city—Catholic and Protestant, fundamentalist and liberal.

Billy and his team decided to work with any Christian group that was willing to help out. This decision enraged many of Billy's staunchest supporters. Others used the opportunity to criticize the movies that the BGEA was producing and showing, arguing that all movies—no matter how Christian they might be—were the devil's tools. Billy was disappointed, but unbowed by such criticism. He told his detractors, "I intend to go anywhere, sponsored by anybody, to preach the gospel of Christ, if there are no strings attached to my message."

The schedule in New York was grueling. Billy preached six nights a week and appeared on all of the popular television and radio talk shows in the country. Other members of his team were also busy preaching and visiting churches around the city. They included Howard Jones, a black pastor from Cleveland, whom Billy had recruited to join the BGEA team as an associate evangelist. Howard joined Ralph

Bell, another black pastor and associate evangelist, whose ancestors had fled slavery and escaped across the border to Canada 150 years before. Billy met with anyone who could further the cause of proclaiming the gospel to as many people as possible. He invited Martin Luther King Jr. to pray the opening prayer at one of the crusade meetings and then spend the weekend with him and his evangelistic team. Several weeks later Billy received a letter from Dr. King.

Dear Dr. Graham:
For many weeks now I have intended writing you, but an extremely busy schedule has stood in my way. I want to express my deep appreciation to you and the members of your staff for your great hospitality on my visit with you in New York. I will long remember the fellowship we enjoyed together. The discussion period that we shared together will remain one of the high points of my life. It was also a great Christian experience to share the platform with you at Madison Square Garden and be a part of such a meaningful service of Christian worship. . . .

I am deeply grateful to you for the stand which you have taken in the area of race relations. You have courageously brought the Christian gospel to bear on the question of race in all of its urgent dimensions. I am sure you will continue this emphasis in all of your preaching, for you, above any other preacher in America, can open the eyes of many persons on this question. Your tremendous popularity, your extensive influence and your powerful message give you an opportunity in the area of human rights above almost any other person that we can point to. Your message in this area has additional weight because you are a native southerner. I am delighted to know that you will be conducting a crusade in Charlotte, North Carolina, on a non-segregated basis. This is certainly a great step. I hope you will see your way clear to conduct an evangelistic crusade in one of the hard-core states in the deep south, even if it is not on as large a scale as most of your crusades. The impact of such a crusade would be immeasurably great.

Although we have a long, long way to go in solving the internal problem of race facing our nation, I still have faith in the future. We are gradually emerging from the bleak and desolate midnight of injustice into the bright and glittering day-break of freedom and justice. This remains true because God is forever at work in His universe. I am convinced now more than ever before that God lives. They that stand against Him stand in a tragic and an already declared minority; they that stand with Him stand in the glow of the world's bright tomorrows.

Billy was encouraged by Dr. King's involvement in the crusade and by his ongoing struggle to see black people take their rightful place in a fully integrated America.

As the crusade in New York City continued, about twenty percent of the crowd attending each night was black. One such person was singer Ethel Waters. Ethel had had a difficult childhood and life, but she responded to Billy's invitation to rededicate herself to Christ. Following her rededication, she came to many meetings to hear Billy preach. Sometimes she agreed to sing her moving solos for the crowd.

The crowd attending the crusade meetings grew each week until the place was filled to capacity. It was not uncommon for eight thousand or more people who could not squeeze into Madison Square Garden to stand in the street outside. A separate platform was built outside from which Billy could preach short messages to those who could not get into the crusade meetings.

Although the New York City Crusade was originally scheduled to end on June 30, 1957, the crowds kept pouring in. Billy and his team decided to extend it. The final meeting on July 20 was held at Yankee Stadium. One hundred thousand people packed the stadium, and another twenty thousand who could not get in stood outdoors listening. It was a blistering hot 95 degrees Fahrenheit outside the stadium. Inside on the platform it was a stifling 105 degrees. Sitting on the platform with Billy was Vice President Richard Nixon, who addressed the crowd and brought greetings from President Eisenhower. It was the first time a political leader of such prominence had attended one of Billy's crusade meetings. The meeting was televised coast to coast across the United States.

At the end of the meeting, a number of crusade team members wondered whether they should make another extension. After a lot of prayer and talking, Billy announced that the crusade would continue on. Back they went to Madison Square Garden, and once again the crowds flocked in each night.

The last "final" meeting of the New York City Crusade was held on September 1, 1957, in Times Square. The police blocked off the surrounding streets, and over seventy-five thousand people turned up to celebrate the end of the longest-ever Billy Graham crusade. In sixteen weeks, over two million people had attended the meetings. Ninety-six million people had seen the meetings on television. Billy Graham was now as famous and as easily recognizable as any movie star in America.

As Billy finished preaching in the New York area, a crisis was brewing in Little Rock, Arkansas. To comply with the *Brown v. Board of Education* Supreme Court ruling in 1954, schools in the Little Rock school district were to be integrated at the start of the 1957 academic year. As a result, nine black students had enrolled to attend Central High, an all-white high school in Little Rock. Several segregationist groups in the city were threatening to hold protests outside Central High and physically block the black students from entering. Arkansas Governor Orval Faubus sided with the segregationists. On the first day of school, September 4, 1957, the governor deployed the Arkansas National Guard to block the black students. The situation in Little Rock made the national news headlines. Billy read about it in the *New York Times.*

The Little Rock School District condemned the governor's actions, and President Eisenhower stepped in to reason with the governor and calm a situation that was quickly polarizing the nation. Orval Faubus stood firm in his position, and the president sought new options to resolve the crisis.

While in New York City one day, Billy received a phone call from Eisenhower. The president explained that he was considering sending federal troops into Little Rock to forcibly integrate Central High and uphold the law. He wanted Billy's advice as a spiritual leader and as a friend.

"Well, Mr. President, I think you have no alternative but to send in troops. The discrimination in Little Rock must be stopped and the law upheld," Billy said.

Dwight Eisenhower thanked Billy for his advice. A half hour later Vice President Richard Nixon also called Billy, seeking his opinion on what should be done in Little Rock. Billy repeated the same advice he had given the president.

Sure enough, on September 24, President Eisenhower sent federal troops to Little Rock to enforce the integration of the schools there and to protect the nine black students enrolled at Central High. He also federalized the entire Arkansas National Guard so that Arkansas's governor no longer controlled them.

After his time in New York, Billy headed home to Montreat. He was never so glad to have the mountain retreat that Ruth had fashioned for the family. There Billy could relax, walk in the woods, pray, and rebuild his physical and emotional strength.

Invitations for Billy to hold crusades flooded in. Billy and the BGEA planned crusades in the Caribbean, California, Texas, and North Carolina for 1958. It was a busy year for Billy, especially since Ruth had another baby in May 1958, a second son whom they named Nelson after Ruth's father. Nelson Graham quickly earned the nickname Ned from his three older sisters and one older brother.

For 1959, the Billy Graham Evangelistic Association booked another overseas crusade, this one in faraway Australia and New Zealand. The planning reached new levels of efficiency and scale. Thousands of neighborhood prayer meetings were organized in the two countries. Five thousand such meetings were held in Sydney, Australia, alone. All sorts of groups, from Aboriginal women's leagues to hospital surgeons, banded together to pray and encourage others to attend the crusade. As with the New York City Crusade, the Australian Crusade was a huge success. Grandstands and auditoriums were filled to overflowing as churches worked together to bring people to the meetings and invite them to join churches afterward.

The team received so many speaking requests in Australia and New Zealand that they had other BGEA associate evangelists speak at the events. Grady Wilson, Leighton Ford (who had married Billy's younger sister Jean), or Englishman Joe Blinco would travel to different cities and hold a series of meetings. On the final night of these meetings, Billy would come to town and preach. The associate evangelists also preached in schools, prisons, dockyards, and factories, blanketing the two countries with the gospel. By the time the Australian Crusade was over, newspapers estimated that one in five New Zealanders had attended a crusade meeting and many more had heard Billy preach on the radio.

Billy returned to the United States via Europe, where he was reunited with Ruth in Paris. The couple traveled on to London, where Billy and Ruth met with Queen Elizabeth II at Buckingham Palace. The queen had been interested in Billy's crusade work since the time he had come to preach at Windsor Castle four years before. Billy gave her a complete report of how his meetings in New Zealand and Australia—over which she was also queen—had gone.

After New Zealand and Australia, Billy's next project was Africa. He chose eleven countries on the African continent to visit: Liberia, Ghana, Nigeria, the Congo, Northern and Southern Rhodesia (now Zambia and Zimbabwe), Kenya, Tanganyika (now Tanzania), Ruanda-Urundi (now Rwanda and Burundi), Ethiopia, and Egypt. Although many people had asked him to come to South Africa, Billy refused to go there. Under the country's apartheid laws, it was illegal to hold meetings with black and white people together.

When he arrived in Africa, Billy saw firsthand the economic, social, and political upheavals taking place on the continent. Colonial domination of Africa was coming to an end, and many former colonies had received their independence or were about to do so. A spirit of nationalism abounded as Africans looked to the future, and a new generation of young leaders was rising up. But the departure of colonial overlords brought with it social upheavals in some countries, especially as people moved from rural areas to the cities in search of economic opportunity. As a student of anthropology, Billy was fascinated by the changes taking place. Yet he also knew that these newly independent countries could go in a number of directions. Communism, Islam, animism, and Christianity vied for the hearts and minds of the African people. For his part, Billy had come to do all he could to promote Christianity and the cause of Christ in Africa.

The reception Billy received in Africa varied from country to country. At his first stop, in Liberia, he was treated as an honored guest of the government. The vice president, Dr. Tolbert, accompanied Billy to all of his meetings, encouraging him to preach openly and refresh the spirit of the people. At his next stop, in Ghana, Billy received quite a different welcome. Ghana had been independent from Great Britain for three years, and the nation's prime minister was not happy that Billy had come. An editorial in the government-sponsored newspaper suggested that Billy should talk only to white people, since they were the "worst form of oppressors and hypocrites history has ever recorded." Billy did not argue with that assessment, but he did want to reach every Ghanaian with the gospel's message of hope and brotherly love. Despite the editorial, large crowds gathered in the cities of Accra and Kumasi to listen to Billy. They also gathered in the Congo and in Nigeria, where he visited a number of cities, among them Kaduna in the north of Nigeria.

While Billy was in Kaduna, a missionary drove him in a Land Rover to a Christian village about twenty miles outside the city. This area of Nigeria was predominantly Muslim, and the missionary related to Billy how the village had been threatened a few years earlier when a small church was erected. A group of machete-wielding thugs invaded the village, intent on destroying it and the people who lived there. The village leader had been a Christian for only four years. He boldly approached the invaders and said, "Young men, our crops are over there. You may burn them if you want. Yonder are our homes. You may tear them down." Opening his robe to bare his neck to the young men, he continued. "Here are our lives. You can kill us if you must. But you cannot take our Christ from us." With that the invaders fled as fast as they had arrived.

Soon the Land Rover approached a group of conical-shaped mud huts and pulled to a stop. The villagers welcomed Billy warmly to their dusty village and showed him the brush arbor—a structure of poles and brush that could hold about one hundred people—that they had built for the meeting with him. Before long the brush arbor was overflowing with local people, some having walked more than fifteen miles to attend the gathering.

As he headed back to Kaduna after the meeting, Billy looked at the conical huts of the village. As the huts faded from view, tears filled his eyes. Billy realized that the Christians of the village had inspired him with their courage and their faith far more than he had encouraged them.

Billy met with the most powerful sultan in Kaduna, the Muslim headquarters for Nigeria. The sultan was already familiar with Billy and his message. "It does not matter what you say," he told Billy. "Within ten years you Christians will be pushed into the sea. We are going to take over Africa."

"That's in God's hands," Billy replied.

"Yes, you are right, it is," the sultan responded.

Billy continued on his tour of African nations, arriving in Ethiopia, which had a population of twenty million people ruled by Emperor Haile Selassie, who was also head of the Ethiopian Orthodox Church. Protestant churches and missionaries were not welcome in the country and were usually barred from speaking in the cities. No one imagined that Haile Selassie would warmly welcome Billy Graham to his country, but he did. The emperor even gave Billy and his team the use of his royal stadium in Addis Ababa in which to hold the crusade meetings. He also ordered that all schools close while the crusade was on and urged the children, including his own grandchildren, to attend.

After visiting Ethiopia, Billy preached in Cairo, Egypt. He then flew to Amman for an eight-day visit to Jordan and Israel. In Jordan he met with the country's leader, King Hussein, and visited many ancient historic sites around the country. In Israel he met with Golda Meir, Israel's foreign minister. He found Mrs. Meir to be gracious and knowledgeable, and he enjoyed her company.

Billy returned to the United States in March 1960. He knew he was privileged to have witnessed so many things and to have met so many wonderful people in Africa. One thing that had impressed him the most was how the human spirit endured when life was very difficult. As he looked around his hometown of Charlotte, North Carolina, with fresh eyes, he knew he had to do more to help bring freedom and equality to black people. He gladly endorsed a biracial committee of one hundred Charlotte citizens to work through the racial divide and bring justice and liberty to every citizen.

The year 1960 was also a presidential election year. Dwight Eisenhower had served two terms as president, and now his vice president, Richard Nixon, was the Republican Party's presidential candidate for the November election. Billy had struck up a close friendship with Nixon over the years. Yet Nixon was running against a talented young United States senator from Massachusetts. The race was tight, and Billy had no idea which way the election would go.

Chapter 13

Change

Billy sat down and stared for a long time at the blank piece of paper. He knew it was a delicate letter to write, and he wanted Jack to know exactly how he felt. He picked up his fountain pen and began writing.

August 10, 1960
The Honorable Jack Kennedy
The United States Senate
Capitol Building
Washington, DC

Dear Senator:
I trust that you will treat this letter in strictest confidence. There is a rumor circulating in the Democratic Party that I intend to

raise the religious issue publicly during the presidential campaign. This is not true. In fact, I would like to commend you for facing it squarely and courageously. . . .

I shall probably vote for Vice President Nixon for several reasons, including a long-standing personal friendship. I am sure you can understand my position. However, if you should be elected President, I will do all in my power to help unify the American people behind you. In the event of your election you will have my wholehearted loyalty and support.

With every good wish, I am cordially yours,
Billy Graham

When he had finished writing, Billy sat back and reflected on the situation. John Fitzgerald Kennedy (Jack, or JFK, as he was known to many people) was a Roman Catholic, only the second Catholic to run for president of the United States. The first was the former governor of New York, Al Smith, who had run and lost against Herbert Hoover in 1928. Al Smith had lost the election, partly because of all the rumors that swirled around the role the pope would play in American politics if Smith won the election for the Democrats. Many well-meaning Americans believed that if Al Smith became president, the pope would move to the United States and rule the country from a fortress in Washington, DC. Those who did not believe the rumors about the pope moving to America simply thought that having a Catholic president was "un-American." Now, thirty-two years later, Jack Kennedy had been nominated for president.

Billy had met Jack Kennedy at several events and liked the man's easy, friendly style. Protestant groups and the Republican Party were now pressuring Billy to stir up the Catholic issue, which would help Richard Nixon win the election. Although Billy liked Nixon and agreed with many of his political positions, he refused to use his influence to spread distrust of Jack Kennedy.

As it turned out on Election Day—November 8, 1960—John Fitzgerald Kennedy was elected the thirty-fifth president of the United States. Following the election Billy told the press, "I don't think Mr. Kennedy's being a Catholic should be held against him by any Protestant. People should judge him on his ability and his character. We should trust and support our new president."

November marked the launch of another project Billy had been contemplating for several years. With the success of *Christianity Today* magazine, Billy began turning his attention to a magazine aimed at everyday Christians rather than the pastors and lay leaders whom *Christianity Today* targeted. He envisaged the magazine having an evangelistic tone containing devotional messages, conversion stories and testimonies, Bible studies, and news of the crusades. Sherwood Wirt, a Presbyterian pastor from California who had also been a journalist, agreed to serve as the founding editor of the magazine. At first Billy was going to call it *World Evangelism*, but then he changed it to *Decision*. The first issue of the magazine came out in November 1960. Nearly 300 thousand copies were printed, and they all sold quickly. Billy was delighted with the look of *Decision* magazine and the way it was received by Christians.

The pace Billy set for himself quickened in the early 1960s. Requests came in from around the world for him to hold crusades. Billy and his associates planned two extended trips to South America during 1962, the first in January and February, the second in September and October.

During the first crusade tour of South America, Billy preached in bullfighting rings, baseball stadiums, and school grounds in Venezuela, Colombia, Ecuador, Peru, and Chile. By the time he returned to the United States, he had preached to over a quarter of a million people.

Back in the United States Billy learned that *Decision* magazine was more popular than ever. George Wilson, business manager for the Billy Graham Evangelistic Association, informed him that the magazine now had more than a million subscribers and that number was growing rapidly each month.

The second trip to South America took Billy to Brazil, Paraguay, Argentina, and Uruguay. Billy also traveled to Mexico. Just before Billy left on his second South American trip, his father, Franklin Graham, died at the age of seventy-four. He had often told Billy how proud he was of him and reminded him of his humble, dairy-farming roots. While saddened by the death of his father, Billy cherished the strong Christian influence his father had exerted on his life. He recalled how he had scoffed when he had overheard his father tell his mother that one of the local men had prayed and asked God to raise up someone from the Charlotte area to preach the gospel to the ends of the earth. Billy would never have guessed that he would be that person.

Other things were changing in the Graham household. While Billy was away preaching for up to six months out of each year, Ruth, along with the aid of a housekeeper and gardener, kept everything running at home. Three years before, the family had moved into their new home on the mountain. They called the homestead Little Piney Cove. Ruth had overseen the construction of the ten-room house, which was built from old logs and timber. Above the large fireplace in the living room, carved in what used to be a diving board, were the German words for the hymn "A Mighty Fortress Is Our God." Rocking chairs sat on the front veranda, which faced out over the rolling hills in the direction of Charlotte.

Every time Billy returned to his mountain homestead, he found that his five children had grown up a little more. This was underscored when Gigi—a seventeen-year-old freshman at Wheaton College—left school to marry a twenty-four-year-old Swiss student named Stephan Tchividjian. The Tchividjian and Graham families had met four years before in Switzerland, and Stephan had made his way to Montreat to woo Gigi. Even though Gigi was young, Billy was happy with the marriage. He felt that Stephan had a solid Christian faith and would make a good husband for his oldest daughter. The two were married in Switzerland in May 1963.

On September 15, 1963, Billy was sickened when he heard the news that a bomb had exploded at the Sixteenth Street Baptist Church, an African American church in Birmingham, Alabama. The explosion killed four girls and injured twenty-two children. Three of the girls killed were fourteen years old, and the fourth was eleven. Billy's heart went out to the girls' parents. He wondered how he would have coped if his own daughters had been killed in such a tragic manner.

Birmingham was one of the most racially divided cities in the United States. In the spring, while Billy had been attending Gigi's wedding in Switzerland, Martin Luther King Jr. had led a protest campaign in Birmingham in the hope of desegregating it. Sit-ins had been held at segregated restaurants and lunch counters, and mass marches had taken place in the streets. Billy saw some television footage of the marches that showed how the city's police force had responded by firing high-pressure water cannons at the protesters and attacking them with police dogs. It was a horrible spectacle to watch, especially when many of the protesters were young students and teenagers. In the course of the confrontation, Martin Luther King had been arrested and thrown into the Birmingham jail, and Billy had bailed King out. Eventually a compromise was reached, and the city of Birmingham agreed to desegregate.

During the Birmingham civil rights protests, the three-story Sixteenth Street Baptist Church had been used as a rallying point for the activities and as a place for King and other civil rights leaders to congregate. Now, five months later, the church had been bombed, killing and wounding innocent children.

Tensions were high in Birmingham following the tragedy. Some of Billy's supporters urged him to cancel the upcoming rally he was planning for Easter 1964. The rally would be fully integrated and would enrage many white people. Billy stood firm. "Though the race question has important social implications, it is fundamentally a moral and spiritual issue," Billy had declared in a 1960 *Reader's Digest* article titled "Brotherhood." "Only moral and spiritual approaches can provide a solution." Billy intended to go to Birmingham because he believed it was both the moral and the spiritual thing to do in the face of the racism that permeated Alabama and other states in the South.

On November 22, 1963, Billy was playing a round of golf with T. W. Wilson, Cliff Barrows, and Lee Fisher at Black Mountain, North Carolina, near his home in Montreat. He had just teed off at the fifth hole when a car screeched to a halt near the men. The manager of the local Christian radio station leaped out of his car, yelling, "The president's been shot. JFK is shot."

Billy left his clubs and rushed toward the car. Within minutes he and his friends were seated at the radio station, reading updates as they came in over the teletypewriter. The minutes seemed to pass like hours—there was no information on the president's condition. Billy then recalled his friend who was a doctor at Parkland Memorial Hospital in

Dallas, where JFK had been taken. He asked TW to call the doctor and find out what was happening.

Meanwhile, Billy went on the air to pray for the Kennedy family. As he read comforting scriptures over the air, TW came to the control room window and held up a scrap of paper against the glass. The note read, "He's dead."

Billy continued to pray. He knew he could not say anything live on the radio until Kennedy's death was officially confirmed. Four minutes later Walter Cronkite broke the news on CBS. "From Dallas, Texas, the flash, apparently official. President Kennedy died at one p.m. Central Standard Time, two o'clock Eastern Standard Time," he announced.

In the studio, Billy's heart sank. He had liked Jack Kennedy, who now was gone—shot by an assassin's bullet. Billy continued to pray on the radio for the Kennedy family and for the nation. He added some prayers for Vice President Lyndon Baines Johnson, who was sworn in as the new president of the United States two hours and eight minutes after President Kennedy's assassination.

Billy attended JFK's funeral the following Monday at St. Matthew's Cathedral in Washington, DC. He was invited to sit with the Kennedy family's friends. It was hard to believe that the president was dead. His murder seemed such a senseless act.

Three weeks later, President Johnson called to invite Billy to visit him at the White House. Billy was glad to go. Accompanied by Grady Wilson, Billy arrived on December 16, 1963. Billy and Grady spent time with Lyndon Johnson, talking and swimming in the White House pool. President Johnson told Billy about his Christian heritage. His grandfather had been a professor of Bible studies at Baylor University, and his great-grandfather, George Washington Baines, had been a frontier evangelist and Baptist minister who was instrumental in converting the famous statesman Sam Houston. The president said he went to church two or three times a week and explained, "No man can live where I live, nor work at the desk where I work now, without needing and seeking the strength and support of earnest and frequent prayer."

The new president had a lot to face: the ongoing battle for full civil rights for black people in the United States as well as the growing fear that the Communists would take over South Vietnam and then the rest of Southeast Asia if the United States did not step in to stop them.

Later that evening Billy and President Johnson talked privately and knelt together in prayer at the end of their meeting. Billy promised to return to the White House often to meet with the president and pray with him.

Chapter 14

Friendship and Disappointment

On Easter Sunday, March 19, 1964, Billy held a large, integrated evangelistic rally at Legion Field Stadium in Birmingham, Alabama. In the lead-up to the rally, members of the Ku Klux Klan had knocked down signs promoting the rally. The state police sent police officers with Billy and his team wherever they went. Officers were also stationed in the rooms around where the team was staying. The police were afraid someone might try to harm Billy or members of his team.

Despite the tension and the police protection, thirty-five thousand people, half of them black and half of them white, sat shoulder to shoulder in the stadium, listening to Billy preach. Billy told them how the gospel could bring peace and goodwill to their city, which had been torn by so much racial strife the previous year. "It is a wonderful thing to gather like this in the city of Birmingham, in the name of Jesus Christ, on Easter Day," Billy said. "Somehow all our problems and difficulties seem not quite so great when we stand at the foot of the cross and hear Him say, 'Father, forgive them, for they do not know what they do.'"

At the end of his sermon Billy gave the usual appeal for people to come to the front to receive Christ. Blacks and whites streamed forward together until a crowd of four thousand people stood in front of the podium. Billy was touched as he watched white counselors begin to counsel and pray with black people while black counselors did the same with white people. It was truly a wonderful sight, and he hoped it would lead to greater harmony in the city of Birmingham and the state of Alabama. The reporters who had come from around the nation to cover the meeting seemed stunned by the outcome. They had not expected to see blacks and whites standing together and interacting cordially with each other. Indeed, the rally at Legion Field Stadium was reported to be the largest integrated audience in the history of Alabama.

A month later, on April 22, 1964, Billy stood backstage watching an audience seated in the new, gleaming-white octagonal building at the New York World's Fair. He listened through a side curtain as his recorded voice boomed out to four hundred people.

They call it a window on the universe, this two-hundred-inch   telescope   atop   Mount

Palomar in Southern California, for on every clear night of the year, an astronomer in the observer's cage high up in the silver dome probes the limitless reaches of outer space. On sensitive photographic film the big two-hundred-inch eye has recorded the light of literally millions of stars. And the end is not yet. For centuries, philosophers and scientists have asked the questions, Where is the end? Where did it all come from? Of course, science does not know the answer to these questions. But we've learned enough through instruments like this to realize that our Earth is a mere grain of sand on the vast seashore of the starry universe.

The audience Billy was watching was viewing the film *Man in the Fifth Dimension.* Billy felt a wave of relief. Just two years before, he had wondered whether the project—the Billy Graham Pavilion—should go ahead at all. Robert Moses, the fair's chief planner, had approached Billy about including the exhibit. The fair's theme was "Peace Through Understanding," and the event was dedicated to "Man's Achievement on a Shrinking Globe in an Expanding Universe." This had interested Billy, but as he had learned more about such a pavilion, he had doubted that the BGEA could make it happen.

The scale of the World's Fair was enormous. At least fifty million people—over one quarter of the population of the United States—were expected to attend during the two years the fair would run. The number seemed overwhelming. If a person spent only twelve minutes at each exhibit, it would take him or her two weeks to see the whole fair. Billy knew that most people wouldn't spend two weeks at the fair. While he planned to make a film using the theme of the event to reach fairgoers, he also wondered how many of them would be willing to spend the twenty-eight minutes necessary to watch it from beginning to end. Not only that, the logistics and cost of staffing a fully air-conditioned pavilion for two years were staggering.

Discouraged by the obstacles, Billy had nearly let the opportunity slip by when Dr. Raymond Edman, president of Wheaton College, wrote and encouraged the project. Dr. Edman reminded Billy that Dwight L. Moody's greatest impact may have been through the extensive campaign he ran in connection with the 1893 Chicago World's Fair.

Billy had decided to move ahead with plans for the pavilion. Now he watched as the audience responded enthusiastically to the state-of-the-art film about the universe and God's love for all people. That made the struggle to get the movie made and the pavilion built on the grounds of the World's Fair in Flushing Meadows, New York City, all seem worthwhile.

For the next two summers, April 22–October 18, 1964, and April 21–October 17, 1965, *Man in the Fifth Dimension* was shown at the Billy Graham Pavilion every hour from 10:00 a.m. to 10:00 p.m. Viewers were offered earphones in a choice of six languages: Russian, German, Spanish, French, Japanese, or Chinese. Afterward, anyone who wanted to stay and talk further about the gospel could talk to a counselor in any of those six languages. The October 1965 issue of *Decision* magazine reported that about one million people had seen the film and that many people, including those who were visiting from behind the Communist Iron Curtain, had heard and responded to the gospel.

In 1964, while the World's Fair was going on, President Johnson signed the Civil Rights Act into law. The act outlawed most forms of racial segregation. Johnson followed up that legislation with the Voting Rights Act on August 6, 1965. This act outlawed discrimination in voting, allowing millions of southern blacks to register to vote for the first time.

Billy was pleased with both pieces of legislation. He admired Lyndon Johnson for his tenacity in making sure the US Congress passed the bills. He also appreciated the deep friendship that had developed between himself and President Johnson. Billy and Ruth had been invited to the White House on several occasions to stay overnight with the Johnsons. Billy and the president would talk openly about their Christian faith. On numerous occasions they knelt together to pray as they had done on Billy's first visit with Lyndon Johnson. During Billy's November 1965 meeting in Houston, Texas, Johnson became the first sitting US president to attend a Graham crusade.

Between the first and second sessions of the World's Fair, Billy kept busy launching crusades on the Hawaiian Islands; in Copenhagen, Denmark; and in Denver, Colorado. In addition to making films and holding crusades, Billy continued writing books. His latest, *World Aflame*, sold one hundred thousand copies in the first three months. At home, Billy and Ruth had entered a new phase of life. In March 1964, at the age of forty-six, Billy became a grandfather when Gigi gave birth to a son, who was named Stephan.

When Lyndon Johnson became president following the assassination of Jack Kennedy, he inherited a difficult situation in Vietnam. President Kennedy had committed US troops as military advisers to the South Vietnamese as they tried to stop a Communist takeover of their country. In an effort to accelerate the progress of the fighting in Vietnam, President Johnson decided to commit American combat troops to the region. By 1966, 429,000 US troops were engaged in a full-on war in Vietnam, a war that was proving to be unpopular at home in the United States. Over Christmas 1966, at the request of General William Westmoreland, Billy, accompanied by George Beverly Shea and Cliff Barrows, went to Vietnam to encourage American troops. Billy traveled all over South Vietnam, sometimes on nail-biting flights that landed at remote, mist-shrouded jungle airstrips. There he preached to the soldiers while Bev Shea serenaded the troops with hymns. For a while Billy even joined up with Bob Hope's show, which was also touring the country and performing for the troops. Referring to entertainer Bob Hope and Billy, soldiers would quip, "He has the hope and you have the faith." While Billy was happy to support American troops, the war itself was depressing. He confided before he left Vietnam, "I leave with more pessimism about an early end to war than when I arrived. . . . I had hoped there would be some formula, but I don't see it. I don't know how it could end."

During 1966 Billy began to realize that he had to slow down a little. At forty-eight years of age, his body was hurting from the constant traveling. He suffered from high blood pressure, kidney stones, and edema. He took the whole month of September off that year and stayed home in Montreat. During that time he walked his second daughter, eighteen-year-old Anne, down the aisle as she married a twenty-eight-year-old Air Force dentist named Daniel Lotz.

During 1967 Billy limited his schedule to five eight-day crusades. He also continued to visit with President Johnson at the White House. Sometimes he and Ruth spent weekends with the Johnsons at Camp David, the presidential retreat in Maryland. Although they didn't talk about it much, Billy could see that growing public opposition to the war in Vietnam was becoming divisive in the country and taking a toll on the president.

Billy was in the midst of a citywide crusade in Sydney, Australia, in April 1968 when he learned that Martin Luther King Jr. had been shot and killed by a sniper as he stood on the second-floor balcony of the Lorraine Motel in Memphis, Tennessee. The news was jarring. Dr. King had given his all to the cause of securing equality and civil rights for African Americans. Now he had paid the ultimate price for that cause.

Billy thought about his relationship with Dr. King. During the New York City Crusade in 1957, they had spent a weekend together. During that time Billy had told Dr. King how he had written in his notebook several years before that eleven o'clock on Sunday morning was the most segregated hour in America. Dr. King had seized on the phrase and used it many times in his speeches and sermons.

There was also the time in 1960 when the two of them traveled together to the Baptist World Alliance in Rio de Janeiro, Brazil. On the way they had stopped off in Puerto Rico for a couple of days to relax. Billy recalled how the two of them swam and talked and prayed together. King had insisted that Billy call him Mike, as his family and close friends did. Billy remembered one poignant exchange the two men had by the pool in Puerto Rico. "I certainly am not going to ever condemn you for your street demonstrations," Billy had stated. "So let me do my work in the stadiums, Mike, and you do yours in the streets." Dr. King had replied, "Billy, I realize that what I'm trying to do will never work until the heart is changed. That's why your work is so important." Billy was impressed with Dr. King's charisma and intellect and his dedication to the cause of racial equality in America.

Now, two months later, on June 5, 1968, Billy was again shocked when he learned that Robert Kennedy, the brother of slain President John Kennedy, had been assassinated in Los Angeles. Millions of Americans wept and began to wonder what was happening to their country. Billy tried to comfort them through his preaching, though he was concerned about the future as well. He felt that the United States was going through its greatest crisis since the Civil War. The mood in the country went from bad to worse. Billy began receiving death threats of his own. He reluctantly ordered an eleven-foot-high fence to be erected around Little Piney Cove. Electronic gates were installed, and the Grahams bought German shepherds to act as guard dogs. These were changes neither Billy nor Ruth could have dreamed of when the couple built their house on the mountain and moved in a decade before.

The year 1968 was also a presidential election year. After doing poorly in the New Hampshire primary, Lyndon Johnson decided not to seek reelection. Instead his vice president, Hubert Humphrey, was the Democratic candidate for president, and former vice president Richard Nixon was the Republican candidate. Nixon was running on a platform to restore law and order to the nation's cities that had been torn by riots and crime.

Billy liked Richard Nixon and had spent many hours with him over the years while Nixon had served as vice president. Nixon came from a Quaker background, and the two men had enjoyed many spiritual conversations about the importance of the Christian faith to individuals and the nation as a whole. The election was a hard fight, but in the end, Richard Nixon narrowly won to become the thirty-ninth president of the United States.

In late December 1968, Billy made a second trip to Vietnam to minister to the troops serving there.

The war was still a quagmire, but following this visit Billy was more upbeat about the possibility that the United States could eventually win.

Billy and Ruth spent the evening of January 19, 1969, at the White House. It was the last night of Lyndon Johnson's presidency. The Johnsons and the Grahams talked and watched a movie together. Billy and Ruth and the Johnsons had grown close over the years. Billy and Ruth had stayed overnight at the White House more than twenty times, spent weekends at Camp David, and visited the Johnsons several times at their ranch in Stonewall, Texas.

The following day Billy prayed at the inauguration of new president Richard Nixon. He was indeed pleased when the president decided to start a regular church service on Sundays at the White House and asked him to conduct the first one.

Billy was in Israel on March 28, 1969, when he was handed a note informing him that Dwight Eisenhower had died of heart failure at age seventy-eight. Billy caught the next available flight back to Washington to attend the former president's funeral.

Meanwhile, back in Montreat, Ruth was helping their third daughter, eighteen-year-old Bunny, prepare for her upcoming marriage to Ted Dienert. Ted was the son of Fred Dienert, the advertising executive who had pestered Billy eighteen years before to put the *Hour of Decision* radio show on the air.

With the three girls all married before their nineteenth birthdays, Ruth and Billy concentrated on their two sons, Franklin and Ned. By now seventeen-year-old Franklin had developed into a rebellious son, determined to show the world he was not going to be a preacher like his father. He embraced the new hippie movement, drank, smoked, and grew his hair long. Ruth struggled to control him. By contrast, eleven-year-old Ned was a quiet and sensitive child, though Ruth confided in Billy that she was concerned about how long he would stay that way, since Franklin teased him mercilessly.

Befriending politicians was also more complicated than Billy could have imagined. He liked Richard Nixon and even invited him to speak at one of his crusades. In 1970 President Nixon appeared onstage with Billy at a crusade meeting in Knoxville, Tennessee. However, during the president's speech a large group of Vietnam War protestors tried to shout him down. It was an uncomfortable moment for Billy, who wanted the focus to be on the Christian message of love and reconciliation, not war and protest.

In 1972 Richard Nixon was elected to another term as president, partly because he promised to bring American troops home and replace them with South Vietnamese soldiers. Nixon was inaugurated for his second term as president on January 20, 1973.

Two day later, on January 22, 1973, news came that Lyndon Johnson had died at his ranch in Texas at the age of sixty-eight. Johnson's funeral services took place on January 25 in the National City Christian Church in Washington, DC, where LBJ had often worshipped as president. Following the state funeral, Lyndon Johnson's body was buried in his family's cemetery in Stonewall, Texas, a few yards

from the house in which he had been born. Billy officiated at his interment in Texas, as he had promised
Lyndon Johnson he would.

Not long after being sworn in for a second term
as president, Richard Nixon began to show another
side, one that Billy had not been aware of during his
years of friendship with the man. The press soon
dubbed Nixon "Tricky Dick." On June 17, 1972,
there had been a burglary at the Democratic National
Committee headquarters at the Watergate office
complex in Washington, DC. Five men were arrested
for the break-in. The FBI later linked them to the
Committee for the Re-Election of the President, the
official fundraising arm of the Nixon campaign.

President Nixon denied any knowledge of the
break-in. However, further investigation by the FBI,
along with reporters Carl Bernstein and Bob Wood-
ward from the *Washington Post* newspaper, indi-
cated otherwise. They discovered that Nixon aides
had committed crimes attempting to sabotage the
Democrats and others in the 1972 election, had lied
about it, and were now trying to cover it up. Nixon
downplayed the incident, which was being called the
Watergate scandal, as mere politics and called the
news articles biased and misleading. By then Billy
did not know what to think. He wanted to believe his
friend, but the evidence against Nixon was mounting.

With the Watergate scandal swirling in the
United States media, Billy left the country to ful-
fill a dream—speaking to an integrated audience of
black, white, and Asian people in South Africa. The

country had an official policy of apartheid—keeping the races separate in all aspects of life. For twenty-six years Christians in South Africa had been asking Billy to come and conduct a crusade there. He refused to go until they could arrange a place where he could talk to people of all races together. In March 1973 that time came.

· On March 13 Billy arrived in Durban, where he spoke twice at the first-ever fully integrated South African Congress on Missions and Evangelism. Then on March 17 he preached at an integrated evangelistic rally at King's Park Rugby Stadium in Durban. Forty-five thousand people of all races jammed the stadium and spilled over onto the rugby field. Billy stood on the platform and looked out over a sea of black and white faces and declared, "Christianity is not a white man's religion. Don't let anybody tell you that it is white or black. Christ belongs to all people!" When Billy gave the invitation to come forward to receive Christ, thirty-three hundred people walked to the front.

The next day the local newspapers declared it to be the largest multiracial crowd to ever gather in South Africa. The headline of one newspaper read, "APARTHEID DOOMED!" Billy hoped so.

Eight days later in Johannesburg, an integrated audience of sixty thousand people packed Wanderers Stadium to capacity. The music for the rally reflected the multiracial nature of the crowd, with everything from a Zulu quartet to white soloists. The rally was carried live on radio across South Africa in

English and Afrikaans. Four thousand people came forward when Billy gave the invitation.

As he left South Africa, Billy hoped the example set by the conference and the evangelistic rallies would have an impact. People of all races could come together and treat each other with love and respect.

Billy almost dreaded returning to the United States. Even in faraway South Africa the newspapers had been full of reports about Nixon and the Watergate scandal. Billy hoped it would all end soon and that the president could get on with dealing with the many issues that faced the country. But when he arrived home Billy found the country still in the grip of political intrigue.

In July 1973 it was revealed that President Nixon had a tape-recording system in his office and had recorded many conversations. A legal tussle then began between the White House and investigators, who demanded the tapes. Nixon refused to release them, claiming presidential authority. The Supreme Court ordered Nixon to turn over the tapes. These condemned him. The tapes revealed that from the beginning Richard Nixon had been aware of what was going on and had orchestrated an elaborate cover-up to keep the truth from investigators and the public. Billy found it hard to absorb this news. It made him physically ill to think that his friend had been so deceptive.

On August 2, 1973, Ruth's father, Dr. L. Nelson Bell, died in his sleep at seventy-nine years of age.

Billy mourned the loss of a wonderful father-in-law and mentor. Nelson had served as a member of the board of directors of the Billy Graham Evangelistic Association and had helped him found *Christianity Today.* Billy knew that no one could fill those shoes in his life again.

Chapter 15

Unlocked Doors to Closed Places

B illy picked up the August 8, 1974, edition of the *New York Times.* The headline splashed across the newspaper's front page said it all: "NIXON RESIGNS. HE URGES A TIME OF 'HEALING'; Ford Will Take Office Today." Billy began reading the article:

Washington, Aug. 8 1974—Richard Milhous Nixon, the 37th President of the United States, announced tonight that he had given up his long and arduous fight to remain in office and would resign, effective at noon tomorrow.

At that hour, Gerald Rudolph Ford, whom Mr. Nixon nominated for vice president last Oct. 12, will be sworn in as the 38th President, to serve out the 895 days remaining in Mr. Nixon's second term.

As he read, Billy felt like someone had punched him in the stomach. It had become obvious to all that Richard Nixon would be impeached by Congress and removed from office if he didn't resign immediately. But Billy just couldn't reconcile the man he was reading about in the *New York Times* with the man he knew and trusted.

Billy was left to do a lot of soul-searching about his relationship with Richard Nixon. Had he been naive? Had he been blind to the man's shortcomings? Had he gotten too close to politics and politicians? Had Nixon used him and their relationship for political purposes? There were no easy answers. All Billy could do was ponder and hope that one day clarity would come.

Despite the setback with Richard Nixon, life went on in the Graham household, and for Billy that meant more crusades. In early October 1974 he traveled to Brazil to hold a crusade in Rio de Janeiro. While there, Billy received some frightening news from his daughter Gigi. She and her growing family had moved to Milwaukee, where her husband was attending graduate school. Ruth was visiting Gigi and the family in Milwaukee when she fell fifteen feet from a tree where she had been rigging up a swing for the grandchildren. She had broken her heel, a rib, and a vertebra, and she was also in a coma. Billy did not know what to do, but Gigi encouraged him to stay where he was. Ruth was in the hospital receiving the best medical care possible.

At the last meeting of the five-day Rio de Janeiro Crusade a quarter of a million people gathered to hear Billy preach, while another fifty million people throughout Brazil watched the meeting on television.

Following the crusade Billy raced home to the United States to be with Ruth, who was out of the coma and slowly recovering from her injuries. On November 8, Billy and Ruth received some sad news. Ruth's mother, Virginia, had died. She had been in poor health for some time after suffering a stroke that left her unable to communicate. Ruth was still on crutches during the funeral. Also, the concussion Ruth had received as a result of her fall from the tree had wiped out much of her short-term memory, making it difficult for her to concentrate for any length of time.

Brighter times were ahead. Ruth's memory slowly returned, while the movie-producing arm of the BGEA produced a blockbuster movie called *The Hiding Place.* The movie told the story of Corrie ten Boom, a Dutch Christian woman who had heroically hidden Jews from the Nazis during World War II and had paid a heavy price for doing so. In addition, Billy's latest book, *Angels*, had become an instant bestseller. Billy did not keep any of the proceeds from these ventures for himself. He still drew a modest salary from the BGEA, but he was delighted that the gospel was reaching people in new and creative ways.

At the next presidential election the Democratic Party candidate was Jimmy Carter, a Christian peanut farmer from Georgia. Carter had served two terms as a Georgia state senator and one term as governor of the state. He was elected the thirty-ninth president on November 2, 1976. Billy was glad to have a professing Christian in the White House, but after Richard Nixon he had learned his lesson never to become too close to a president. Instead, he concentrated on new opportunities ahead for him and the Billy Graham Evangelistic Association.

In 1972 Billy had been introduced to a brilliant Hungarian-born doctor named Alexander Haraszti. Dr. Haraszti was a medical doctor and also held a doctorate in linguistics and a degree in theology. He spoke eight languages, but more importantly, he had a passion for preaching the gospel in his homeland, which he had left in 1956. Hungary was one of the Communist countries of Europe's Eastern Bloc, which was under the domination of the Soviet Union. As a result, religious activity in the country was monitored and regulated. Still, Dr. Haraszti did what he could to help Christians in his home country. He translated Billy's *Peace with God* book into Hungarian, and he worked behind the scenes with the many contacts he still had in Hungary to get Billy Graham invited to preach in the country.

In August 1977 Dr. Haraszti's efforts paid off. The Hungarian government granted Billy the opportunity to preach in the country, provided he met several conditions. Billy was forbidden to mention politics, the entire evangelistic team had to stay where they were directed to stay and disclose where they would be at all times, and there was to be absolutely no advertising of the meetings. Even the pastors in officially approved churches could not announce that Billy Graham was coming to Hungary.

Billy prayed hard about the upcoming trip. He felt that this mission could help break down Communism in Hungary and lead to more rights for Christians—but only if the trip went well. Ruth traveled with him, as did Dr. Haraszti. As Billy preached in churches, he discovered that his message—ably translated by Alexander Haraszti—was spreading across Hungry via tape recordings. On September 4, 1977, Billy was in Budapest to speak at an unadvertised Baptist youth camp. No one knew how many people would come, but over fifteen thousand Hungarians poured into the campground. Billy watched in awe as people clambered up the nearby hillside and climbed trees to see him preach. It felt like he was witnessing a modern-day version of the Sermon on the Mount. The successful trip paved the way for Billy to preach in other Eastern Bloc countries. The following year, Billy traveled to Poland.

On May 7, 1980, the airplane carrying Billy and Ruth, Ruth's brother Clayton, and her sisters Rosa and Virginia, touched down in Beijing. The trip to China was the fulfillment of a dream for Ruth. She and her siblings were going back to see Tsingkiang, where their father had worked as a medical missionary, and to show Billy where Ruth had been born. The trip had been arranged with the help of Richard Nixon, who had continued to make trips to China after he left the presidency and who had many high-level contacts in the country. Although stunned by the revelations of the Watergate scandal, Billy had remained friends with Nixon.

After several days of sightseeing in the Chinese capital, the group moved on to Tsingkiang, located about three hundred miles northwest of Shanghai. As they pulled up to the old mission compound where the Bell family had lived, Billy could see that this was an emotional moment for his wife. Ruth had not seen the place for forty-three years. The two-story house the family had lived in was dilapidated but still standing, as were the hospital where she was born and the mission school she had attended as a young child. As they walked around the compound, Billy imagined Dr. Bell at work. Dr. Bell had been the supervisor of what was then the largest mission hospital in the world. Some residents of the town still remembered the Bell family and spoke fondly of them and the work Dr. Bell had done at the hospital.

While it was emotional and nostalgic for the Bell siblings to be in the place they had grown up, it was a moment of understanding for Billy. For the first time he was able to see and experience the things his wife had told him about from her youth.

As the trip to China drew to a close, Billy felt challenged. The people he had met in China were warm and friendly, but so many of them had no knowledge of the gospel. Yet those people he talked to about it were genuinely interested. When he got back to the United States, Billy and his entire organization began to pray that God would open a door for them to go to China.

In the presidential election of 1980, Jimmy Carter lost to Ronald Reagan, the Republican candidate who had been a former Hollywood actor and governor of California. Billy had known Reagan for over twenty-five years, and he felt that Reagan was a good choice to lead the United States as the fortieth president.

Morrow Graham died on August 14, 1981, a few months before her ninetieth birthday. Billy wept when he received the news. Of all the people he had ever known, his mother had had the greatest impact on him. Billy remembered that she was the one who had encouraged him to go to Wheaton College and how every morning at ten she and Billy's father would kneel to pray for him. Now she was gone, the last of Billy's and Ruth's parents to die. Billy was grateful that his mother had lived long enough to see the results of many of her prayers.

In 1982 Billy was given another opportunity to visit Russia. In 1959 Billy, accompanied by Grady Wilson and Bill Jones, an American businessman, had traveled to Moscow in the Soviet Union. Bill Jones had made many trips to the country before, sometimes carrying Bibles with him to give to Christians, and he had wanted Billy to see the place for himself. The men had traveled as tourists, since the Soviet Union was officially an atheist country and Christians, let alone an international evangelist, were forbidden to preach there. That trip had been eye-opening for Billy. Wherever he went, some people seemed to recognize him and secretly drew a cross, whether on the ground, a misty window, or their hand to indicate to him that they were Christians. The Communist government tightly controlled the country, and the Russian Orthodox Church and the Baptist Church were the only two Christian denominations allowed. Even then, the government had to approve every decision they made. While Billy abhorred Communism, he was impressed by the spirit of the Russian people who endured under such a harsh political system. He wanted to come back one day and preach, though that did not seem likely.

Twenty-two years after that trip to Moscow, the Russian Orthodox Church was planning a conference, which was called the "World Conference of Religious Workers for Saving the Sacred Gift of Life from Nuclear Catastrophe," to be held in Moscow in May 1982. Working with contacts they had in the Soviet Union, Alexander Haraszti and two other men managed to arrange for Billy to be officially invited to the conference as an observer and to address the conference attendees. Billy eagerly accepted the chance to go back to Moscow—and this time to speak to and share with Christians.

Billy's plan to attend the conference in Moscow drew a lot of criticism for the American press. He was accused of being a puppet of the Soviet government, which the press believed would use his presence for propaganda purposes. Billy knew that the US State Department had deep reservations about his visit, and the newspapers were reporting that President Reagan hoped he would reconsider his decision. Even some BGEA board members wondered whether Billy was doing the right thing. Despite the criticism and reservations about the trip, Billy held firm. He believed that this was a door into a previously closed place that God had unlocked for him, and he intended to step through it.

Billy set out for Moscow at the beginning of May 1982. The Sunday before he left, he had lunch with Vice President George Bush and President and Mrs. Reagan. During their lunch President Reagan took Billy aside and told him that he was glad he was going to the Soviet Union. This made Billy feel a lot better about his decision.

The conditions Soviet officials set for Billy were strict. Billy was allowed to preach only in state-approved Russian Orthodox or Baptist churches. However, within those restrictions Billy was free to say whatever he wanted, and he preached the same gospel he had preached in countless other cities around the world. On May 11 he delivered a speech at the conference titled "The Christian Faith and Peace in a Nuclear Age." At the conference Billy became friends with Patriarch Pimen, the head of the Russian Orthodox Church.

While in Moscow, Billy was invited to the Kremlin, where he met with Boris Ponomarev, a member of the Politburo, the Soviet Union's governing body, and chairman of the Foreign Affairs Committee of the Supreme Soviet of the USSR. The two men spoke cordially but forthrightly about a number of issues, such as the barriers between the two countries and the treatment of Christians in Russia. As he liked to do when he met world leaders, Billy talked about his personal Christian faith. Following their meeting, Ponomarev took Billy on a private tour of the Kremlin.

Remarkably, just two years later, Billy returned to the Soviet Union, this time with permission to conduct full crusades in four cities: Moscow, Leningrad, Novosibirsk, and Tallinn in Estonia. Accompanying Billy on the crusade tour was a young minister who held a special place in his heart—his son, who was now the Reverend Franklin Graham. Franklin had put his rebellious ways behind him and committed himself to following Jesus Christ. Although the numbers attending his meetings in the Soviet Union were far smaller than the huge crowds he was accustomed to in his crusades, Billy felt the meetings were worthwhile. A new wind of religious freedom was beginning to blow in the Soviet Union.

Following his return to the United States, Billy began to rely on Franklin more and more. He realized that it was time to encourage other younger men and women to reach the next generation with the gospel. Three years later this was underscored when his close friend and associate Grady Wilson died from a heart condition. Billy preached at Grady's funeral on November 3, 1987, just four days before Billy turned sixty-nine years old. As he stood looking at Grady's coffin, he recalled the first time they had met at Mordecai Ham's evangelistic meetings in Charlotte.

After the funeral many people marveled at how Billy and Grady had worked side by side for over fifty years, yet it had seemed perfectly natural to Billy. They were two boys from North Carolina who had spent their lives traveling the world preaching the gospel. As he looked around, Billy saw T. W. Wilson,

Grady's older brother, who was still an associate evangelist with the BGEA, and George Beverly Shea, now seventy-eight years old, who still sang at many of Billy's crusades. They had all started out as young men with a common goal, and Billy had no doubt they would remain committed to each other until the end.

Chapter 16

A National Treasure

It was 2:30 p.m. on a cloudless, sunny day in Los Angeles, October 15, 1989. Billy Graham, three weeks short of his seventy-first birthday, stood outside Mann's Chinese Theatre on Hollywood Boulevard. For once he felt a little out of place, not because he was in Hollywood, but because of the reason the crowd of twenty-five hundred people who stood on the sidewalk in front of him and spilled out into the street had gathered. The crowd was there to celebrate the unveiling of a Hollywood star marking Billy Graham's place on the famous Hollywood Walk of Fame. Billy would be joining famous entertainers like Charlie Chapman, Mickey Rooney, and Bob Hope, all of whom had stars on the walk.

Once the pink star was unveiled, Billy spoke. "Some people may ask why I would agree to have my name put on the Hollywood Walk of Fame. Isn't that kind of egotistical?" Billy paused for a moment before continuing. "It may be for some, but the reason I agreed to do this is that I thought one day some little child will walk along this street and look down and say, 'Mommy, who is Billy Graham?' That mother would be able to tell her child, 'Billy Graham was a minister of the gospel of Jesus Christ. Let me explain to you what that gospel is.'"

Someone in the crowd asked whether Billy minded his name being permanently embossed on a boulevard along with a large number of "sinners." Billy didn't miss a beat. "We're all sinners," he replied. "Everybody you meet all over the world is a sinner. The word *sin* means you've broken with the laws of God. We've all done that. So I couldn't condemn Hollywood Boulevard any more than any other place."

As usual when at such events, Billy preached the gospel to all who were present. This was something he'd been doing for over fifty years, and he intended to continue for as long as his health would allow.

Two years later, in September 1991, Billy preached on the Great Lawn of New York City's Central Park. Over a quarter of a million people showed up to listen to him, making it the single largest religious gathering in the history of New York City—and Billy's single largest event in North America.

A year later Billy was forced to think about slowing down. He began to notice that his body was not acting quite the way he wanted it to. Sometimes he stumbled even though the path was level, or he reached for a glass of water but knocked it over instead. During a visit to the Mayo Clinic in Minnesota, Billy was diagnosed with Parkinson's disease. It was an unexpected diagnosis, since there was no history of the disease in his family. The doctor explained to Billy that Parkinson's disease slowly destroys the brain cells that control muscles. As the disease progressed, Billy's hands and legs would start to tremble, and then larger muscle groups would be harder for him to control. Billy took the news well. He often preached that suffering is a part of the human condition that each person will experience at some stage of life. He adjusted his schedule some to account for the disease but kept on going.

In October 1992, Billy was back in Moscow for a citywide crusade. It was hard for him to grasp the tremendous changes that had taken place there since his first visit in 1959. A little less than a year before, the Communist Soviet Union had collapsed. The old, repressive government was swept aside, and a new day had dawned in Russia, not only politically, but also spiritually. The old atheist stance of the Communists was gone. Russians were now able to freely attend church, worship, and evangelize. The Moscow Crusade was held in the old Olympic stadium that seated thirty-eight thousand people. From the start the facility was filled to overflowing. On Saturday night, the last meeting of the crusade, Billy was moved to tears as he listened to the Russian Army Chorus, formerly the Soviet Red Army Chorus, sing "Battle Hymn of the Republic" in English. Even in his wildest dreams Billy could not have imagined such a thing.

When Billy gave the invitation at the end of his sermon, at least twenty thousand people, nearly half the audience, came forward to receive Jesus Christ. Billy could scarcely take in what was happening. It was the single highest percentage of people ever to respond at a crusade meeting in his entire career as an evangelist.

By now Billy had reached a time in his life when many of his old friends and colleagues were dying. More often than not, he was asked to preach at their funerals. In 1993 he officiated at the funeral of former first lady Pat Nixon. A year later on April 27, 1994, he officiated at Richard Nixon's funeral on the grounds of the Nixon Library in California. While the Watergate scandal had marred his relationship with the former president, the two had managed to move beyond it and stay friends. Now his friend of over forty-four years was dead at the age of eighty-one.

The nation also called on Billy Graham to help heal national wounds. In 1995 Billy spoke at the memorial service following the bombing by domestic terrorists of the Alfred P. Murrah Federal Building in downtown Oklahoma City. One hundred sixty-eight people died, and another six hundred eighty were injured in the blast.

Billy still spoke at crusades, but the gatherings were shorter now and less frequent. In 1995 he spoke in San Juan, Puerto Rico; Toronto, Canada; and Sacramento, California. The following year he spoke in Minneapolis-St. Paul, Minnesota; and Charlotte, North Carolina.

During 1996, Billy's son Franklin was made vice chairman of the board of directors of the Billy

Graham Evangelistic Association. It was decided that he should be Billy's successor when Billy became too frail to carry on. In May of the same year, Billy and Ruth Graham received the Congressional Gold Medal in a ceremony held at the Capitol in Washington, DC.

Billy continued to find innovative ways to reach out to people. In 1998 he spoke at a TED talk, a global conference for a large group of scientists and philosophers. His message was simple. Great scientific minds can create new things like cell phones, CT scanners, and many other wonderful devices that can make life better for people. These innovations, however, can also be used for great evil. Only God can change the human heart. It was the same message Billy had set forth in the movie *Man in the Fifth Dimension* at the World's Fair in New York City thirty-four years before.

By now Billy Graham was considered a national treasure by many Americans. In 2000, former first lady Nancy Reagan presented him with the Ronald Reagan Freedom Award.

The following year, on September 14, 2001, in the aftermath of the September 11 terrorist attacks on the World Trade Center in New York City and the Pentagon in Alexandria, Virginia, Billy was invited to speak at a national church service held at the National Cathedral in Washington, DC. The service was attended by President George W. Bush and many other past and present American and world leaders.

Three months later, Billy was once again in Washington. This time he was to receive an honorary knighthood from the Queen of England. Sir Christopher Meyer, the British ambassador to the United States, performed the investiture ceremony on behalf of Queen Elizabeth II. The guests at the ceremony were told that Billy Graham was receiving the honor for his "huge and truly international contribution to civic and religious life over sixty years." And it was true. By now Billy had preached to live audiences of nearly 215 million people in more than 185 countries and territories. He had also reached hundreds of millions more through radio, television, and film. Over the years he had met with countless political leaders, from kings, queens, and emperors to presidents, premiers, and prime ministers, and with business, civic, and religious leaders. In each of these meetings Billy had sought to tell the leader what God personally meant to him. As an evangelist, Billy Graham had truly gone to the ends of the earth to preach the gospel.

Most former presidents of the United States have their own libraries, which are more like official museums depicting them and the times in which they lived. May 31, 2007, was a special day for Billy. He was present at the dedication of the Billy Graham Library in Charlotte, North Carolina. Billy maneuvered his walker across the stage and sat down. Beside him was the forty-thousand-square-foot library building styled after a dairy farm barn. Behind him was the two-story brick house where he had grown up. The house had been moved four miles down the road to the site of the library. It was now filled with Graham family memorabilia.

Sitting at Billy's left were three former presidents: Jimmy Carter, Bill Clinton, and George H. W. Bush. One by one they took turns at the podium telling the audience their recollections of Billy Graham long before they became presidents. Jimmy Carter recalled living in Sumter County, Georgia, when the BGEA asked him to lead an integrated crusade based on a movie presentation. It was the first event of its kind in the county, and it hastened the end of racial segregation there. Carter said of Billy, "He was constantly broadminded, forgiving, humble in his treatment of others. He has reached out equally for opportunities to serve God to all people, black or white, American or foreign, man or woman. My testimony today is that I am just one of tens of millions of people whose spiritual lives have been shaped by Billy Graham."

Bill Clinton spoke next. He recalled Billy breaking down racial barriers in Arkansas. "Almost fifty years ago, when I had been a Christian for just about three years, my Sunday school teacher took me to Little Rock to hear Billy Graham's crusade. The schools were closed because of Little Rock's Central High School's integration crisis, and I had exactly the same experience Jimmy Carter did. The White Citizens Council in Little Rock tried to convince, even to pressure, Billy Graham and all of his people to preach to a segregated audience. . . . [Billy] told them that if [they] insisted on that, he would cancel the crusade and tell the whole world why. . . . So here we were with neighborhood after neighborhood in my state on the verge of violence, and yet tens of thousands of black and white Christians [were] there together in a football stadium, and when he issued the call at the end of the message, thousands came down holding hands, arm-in-arm, crying. It was the beginning of the end of the old South in my home state. I will never forget it."

George H. W. Bush, father of George W. Bush, was the last of the three presidents to speak. He said, "The moral awakening which Billy helped to ignite, starting in America, but then spreading like wildfire across the country, and ultimately . . . around the entire world, was also the same spark that ignited hope and kept the embers burning in faraway places—behind an Iron Curtain. And just as there was a coalition of free nations who stood together in the face of this geopolitical threat, so too was there a brotherhood of great spiritual leaders, such as our honoree and Pope John Paul II, who with unaffected charisma and purity of purpose played a decisive role in solving the world crises of our time."

President Bush then spoke about how much Billy Graham's kindness and counsel had meant to four generations of his family. He began to weep, and the audience waited for him to compose himself before continuing.

George Beverly Shea and Cliff Barrows stood at the podium together. Bev, who was now ninety-eight years old, sang his signature hymn, "How Great Thou Art," and recounted how he had first introduced it to the American audience at the 1957 New York City Crusade at Madison Square Garden. Cliff Barrows spoke of the first time the members of the BGEA got together in Charlotte fifty-seven years before.

Then Billy stood up to speak. He had long, snow-white hair now, and he gripped the podium for balance. But there was still something of the old evangelist who could connect with his audience. Billy's first comment attracted a laugh. "I feel like I have been attending my own funeral," he said. "Listening to all those speeches, I know they all meant it. But I feel terribly small and humbled by it all, and I feel I don't deserve it because it's been a whole team of people who have worked together, prayed together, traveled together, believed that God was going to do wonderful things together.

"I've been here to this library once before, and I am overwhelmed. My one comment when I toured was, 'There's too much Billy Graham.' You know my whole life has been to please the Lord and to honor Jesus, not to see me—not to think of me. You've already heard from Bev Shea and Cliff Barrows, and they've been a major part of my ministry and work. I think the press and the media chose me to write about, but I think of all the people who worked and prayed through the years, and I want to thank them all."

Billy then went on to talk about Ruth. "I miss terribly today my wife, Ruth. She's been in bed now for six months. I go in to be with her several times a day to see her and remember all the great things we've shared together. Today I want to honor her and tell you how much I love her and tell you what a wonderful woman she has been. . . .

"This building behind me is just a building, it's an instrument, it's a tool for the gospel. The primary thing is the gospel of Christ. . . . I pray that God will use this to speak to many people who come through this facility, and I need your prayers and I want to thank you again for coming today."

Two weeks after the Billy Graham Library dedication, Ruth Bell Graham died at eighty-seven years of age, surrounded by her family. Billy held her hand until the end. Ruth's body was laid to rest in a simple plywood casket that had been made by prison inmates. The casket cost $200 and was lined with a mattress pad. Ruth had requested the casket, and Billy had approved. He felt it stood as a symbol of Ruth's life. Ruth had always been a simple person with simple tastes, who cared for the downtrodden and those in need.

At the funeral, Ruth's older sister Rosa spoke about growing up in China and how Ruth and Billy met. Billy stood and spoke as well, thanking everyone for their love and support and greeting his nineteen grandchildren and numerous great-grandchildren. He told them that he was "looking forward to the . . . next service here," when he also would be freed from his aging body. He assumed it would not be long. Little did he know he had a long way yet to go.

Chapter 17

Life and Legacy

It took Billy a long time to adjust to life without Ruth. She had made their log cabin at Little Piney Cove a home, and now the place seemed empty without her around. Still, Billy carried on as best he could. But his world was narrowing as his Parkinson's disease progressed, and he suffered from other illnesses and ailments as well. He began to go blind and became hard of hearing, which made it difficult for him to participate in many events and he was forced to withdraw from everyday public life.

As the years passed, more old friends and colleagues passed away, among them George Beverly Shea. The man Billy had originally recruited sixty-nine years before to sing on the *Songs In the Night* radio show died at the age of 104. He had sung at just about every one of Billy's crusades, made seventy records, won a Grammy award and a Life-time Achievement award. But to Billy he was simply a dear friend first. Billy insisted on attending Bev Shea's funeral, even though he was wheelchair bound, and on oxygen.

As Billy approached his ninety-fifth birthday, the Billy Graham Evangelical Association decided to celebrate Billy's life and legacy in a special way. In November 2013 the BGEA launched *My Hope America with Billy Graham*, a video evangelism course designed for Christians to use in small group contexts in their homes and churches. The videos show highlights of Billy's teaching and preaching, and stories from the lives of those who have been changed by the Gospel message.

Billy's health continued to decline as he turned ninety-nine years old on November 7, 2017. He spent many hours in bed at Montreat, North Carolina, listening as others read the Bible aloud to him.

Finally, on Wednesday, February 21, 2018, Billy Graham died peacefully at his home, nine months short of his hundredth birthday. In addition to his five children, he left 44 grandchildren and six great-grandchildren to mourn his death.

Millions of people around the world joined the Graham family in honoring their father and grandfather. From February 28 through March 1, 2018, Billy Graham became the fourth private citizen in United States' history to lie in honor in the U.S. Capitol Rotunda in Washington, D.C. There, thousands of people came to pay their last respects to him.

It was then time for Billy Graham's final earthly journey. His body was taken from Washington D.C.

to the Billy Graham Center in Charlotte, North Carolina. There, on March 2, in a huge open tent, similar to the one Billy preached in during his famous
Los Angeles crusade sixty-nine years before, 2,300
invited guests attended his funeral service. Many
Christian dignitaries were there from over fifty countries, along with the President and Vice-President of
the United States and their wives.

Billy's lone surviving sibling, his 85-year-old sister Jean, spoke first. She was followed in turn by
each of his children, who shared memories of their
father and the legacy he had left them. Next, pastors from around the world shared how Billy Graham had conducted crusades in their countries and
testified to the worldwide impact of his ministry.

Perhaps Boz Tchividjian summed up Billy Graham's life best in an article he wrote for the *Washington Post* honoring his grandfather Daddy Bill, as
he lovingly referred to him.

What I will perhaps cherish most about
Daddy Bill is that he taught me the meaning of humility. Toward the end of his life,
one of his favorite Bible verses was, "May I
never boast except in the cross of our Lord
Jesus Christ, through which the world has
been crucified to me, and I to the world" (Gal.
6:14). The verse was typed out in large font
and hanging in various places in his bedroom
and bathroom. He recognized that his life and
leadership was not about himself. In fact, he
always felt uncomfortable when the focus of

any conversation was himself or his accomplishments. More often than not, Daddy Bill shifted the subject away from himself and toward Jesus.

I've been in the room when Daddy Bill called and spoke to the President of the United States, and later got up to pull the chair out for the housekeeper, whom he regularly invited to join him and Ruth for dinner. Here was a man who was no less interested in the lives of taxi drivers, housekeepers and waitresses than presidents, prime ministers and members of royalty.

Following the funeral service, Billy's body was laid to rest beside that of his beloved wife Ruth in the Prayer Garden on the northeast side of the Billy Graham Library.

Aikman, David. *Billy Graham: His Life and Influence.* Nashville: Thomas Nelson, 2007.

Cornwell, Patricia. *Ruth, a Portrait: The Story of Ruth Bell Graham.* Colorado Springs: WaterBrook Press, 1998.

Frady, Marshall. *Billy Graham: A Parable of American Righteousness.* Boston: Little Brown, 1979.

Gibbs, Nancy, and Michael Duffy. *The Preacher and the Presidents: Billy Graham in the White House.* New York: Center Street, 2007.

Graham, Billy. *Just As I Am: The Autobiography of Billy Graham.* San Francisco: HarperSanFrancisco, 1997.

Wellman, Sam. *Billy Graham: The Greatest Evangelist.* Reprint, Uhrichsville, OH: Barbour Publishing, 2012.

Wilson, Grady. *Count It All Joy.* Broadman, 1984.

Billy Graham Library Dedication: May 31, 2007, accessed at http://www.c-spanvideo.org/program/BillyG.

Janet and Geoff Benge are a husband and wife writing team with more than thirty years of writing experience. Janet is a former elementary school teacher. Geoff holds a degree in history. Together they have a passion to make history come alive for a new generation of readers.

Originally from New Zealand, the Benges make their home in the Orlando, Florida, area.

HEROES OF HISTORY are available in paperback, e-book, and audiobook formats, with more coming soon! Unit Study Curriculum Guides are available for each biography.

www.EmeraldBooks.com